Pathways to Perfect Living

Vernon Howard

NEW LIFE FOUNDATION
Pine, Arizona 85544

Library of Congress Catalogue Card Number: 69-55447

ISBN 0-911203-35-4
New Life Foundation
PO Box 2230
Pine AZ 85544
(520) 476-3224

It is not far, it is within reach,
Perhaps you have been on it since you
were born and did not know.

Walt Whitman

How This Book Can Help You

In this book you will discover a gratifying new Way for success in daily perfect living. The Path this Way follows is like floating serenely down a broad and beautiful river. There is no need for anxious effort; you need only relax and permit yourself to be carried forward.

This secret is generally considered to be *rare, available only to a few*. However, if you truly wish this power and wisdom for perfect living above all else, you can be one of the select few to receive its riches through this book. You can experience:

    1. *A wonderful release from living with a self that was previously burdened and confused.*

    2. *An entirely new way to meet and solve daily difficulties.*

    3. *Total relief from pains and guilts and anxieties arising from past mistakes.*

    4. *An amazing self-command, in which you live your own life, free from society's pressures and frustrations.*

    5. *The ending of fear, tension, worry.*

    6. *A refreshing newness and happiness in living which nothing can take away from you.*

    7. *Invisible Perfect Guidance, which faultlessly directs your steps toward your own best interests.*

What is the origin of principles of Perfect Living? They come from what is known as the High Places. On the human level, they are a blending of ancient and modern wisdoms from East and

West. These truths are simplified into programs and made practical for modern men and women in daily life. This book includes many case histories of those who sought and found the power for perfect living from the High Places.

Let's imagine that you ask me, *How can I make the most of this book?* I reply, *Read it with a mind that wishes to discover something entirely different and workable for perfect living.* With this receptive attitude, the next few weeks could mark the great turning point of your life. The day may well come when you will exclaim, *Amazing! Why didn't I know this before? Well, never mind; I am on my way up at last.*

So, let's explore together these marvelous secrets of new power, which deliver daily success for your perfect living.

VERNON HOWARD

Contents

The case of a rich man in chaos. Hidden dynamic facts about your mind. Why an intellectually conditioned mind fails to protect. The marvelous third way of thinking successfully. Let your day always be an adventure. How to start. How mental miracles happen. The need for a fresh mind. How to change unwanted conditions. A marital problem solved. The true approach never fails. How to break through the roadblocks of life. How dreams may be made to come true. How a businessman won success. How grief can vanish in a flash. The importance of the cosmic command, "be still."

How one man banished nervousness. The shocking truth about human and cosmic laws. How to let cosmic powers work for you. How Richard turned cruelty into kindness. Three extraordinary principles for self-enrichment. How to conquer your destructive, negative emotions. How emotional energy was saved for useful work. Everything is in your favor for winning your goals. How a guilt complex was healed. How to be free from your error of self. What self-awareness means. Transcendental living is a cheery adventure. Cosmic principles of personal security.

How to live from your inner essence. How to separate truthful ways from false ways. How perfect

How to solve the mystery of authentic self-transformation. How to penetrate the mystery of invisible guidance. You will solve the mystery of how to end anxiety. Exciting experiences you may expect. How a salesman acquired valuable self-knowledge. How to dissolve shock and disappointment. The correct response to external events. How to let accusations work to your benefit. Secrets for instant help for yourself. How you can attune to hear cosmic truth. When you don't know what to do about a problem. How to cope with compulsive thoughts.

How loss can mean gain. How true riches come to you. Cosmic wisdom is within your mind. The conference of the birds. How to become a truly new person. How to be humiliated and appreciate it. How accepted humiliation enriches. The advantages of destroying your illusions. Your insight banishes all human struggling. How to attain authentic love and peace.

How one man conquered his problems. You can command your own life. How blunders can turn into advancements. How to be free of damaging ideas. Solving the problem of security. A wonder-working statement to make. How to simplify your day. How to win new strength and self-confidence. The sure cure for all human problems.

The alarm clock expert. The effective simplicity of cosmic strength. Sure steps toward supreme success. Your new kind of victory. How to refresh your day. You can certainly succeed. Two dynamic programs for self-advancement.

1

Your Wonderful Power
for Perfect Living

There was once a community of desert dwellers who were all afflicted by a painful sickness. Because the sickness was so severe, it made them quarrelsome and irritable. In an attempt to forget the pain, they invented a wide variety of distractions, including alcohol and shallow amusements.

But their major escape from pain was to engage in a gigantic stage performance, in which they flattered and deceived each other. This was done by wearing masks which gave the appearance of goodness and sincerity, but behind the masks, they were quite vicious in exploiting each other. Men who appeared kindly quite easily fooled women who appeared glamorous; women who appeared devoted had no problem in fooling men who appeared wise.

The performance, being pain and strain in itself, only doubled the sickness of the people, but it was the only thing they knew to do.

One day a physician appeared with a wonderful message. Holding up a bottle containing a unique kind of liquid, he addressed the sufferers: *"Here is the sure cure for your illness. There is plenty for all who really want it. But you must willingly receive and carry out my instructions."*

The physician then went into detail, saying, *"You must honestly see how dreadfully sick you really are. Then, you must give up your stage performances, for they prevent recovery. Also, you must set aside all your other old and useless medicines. There is*

1

only one cure for your illness, which I now give to you. Treasure it above all else, and apply it individually, for in no other way can you become whole. Apply a drop of this medicine over your heart every day. Let nothing distract you from faithful application. Then, you will know what it means to be healthy and happy human beings."

Leaving the bottle with them, the physician went away. Immediately, the men fell into childish quarrels. One of them demanded that they organize the physician's teachings, with himself as their leader. Another wanted to meet once a week to praise the physician, but another angrily insisted upon twice a week. Also, they quarreled violently over the meaning of the physician's instructions, each insisting that he alone knew the true interpretation. They paused in their hostility toward each other only long enough to proclaim publicly how much they loved each other.

And so, with all the frantic activities, no one remembered to apply the liquid. Everyone remained just as sick as he was before.

However, in time, two or three individuals felt themselves strangely affected by the words of the physician. They began to see them in a new way. Though sick themselves, they detected the ring of truth in what they had heard. And so, unlike the others, they applied the medicine over their hearts and became well.

THE AMAZING TRUTH ABOUT MYSTIC WISDOM

The wonderful medicine which can cure anyone of every form of illness is called esoteric wisdom.

All this is not really complicated. It is quite simple. How would you like to learn to use your mind so as to live the way you really like? *That* is what esotericism is all about.

To be an expert in the ways of your mind is the most profitable occupation on earth. People ask, "But why should I deeply study my mind?" Well, why study science or finance or health? Because they make life intelligent and comfortable. If this is so on the everyday level of science and finance, how much more so when it comes to psychic health.

Esotericism is not merely something interesting and helpful; it is an absolute necessity for man's individual and social survival. Why a necessity? Because you can walk into any home or office and say to whomever you meet, "Life is a suppressed nightmare," and he will know exactly what you mean. Since it is only painfully pressured people who make war and create chaos, esotericism can relieve their inner pressures and so change the exterior world.

How Norma Was Cleared of a False Sense of Guilt

I recall Norma W. whose introduction to esoteric ideas uplifted her life in an astonishing way. Her particular problem was a false sense of guilt. In an effort to relieve the pressure, she never said *no* to those who asked for her time, energy and even her money—and the asking was endless. She resentfully felt that she was being more of a sucker than an angel, but did not know how to break out.

I introduced Norma to esoteric principles, which revealed that her first duty in life was to her own inner awakening. From that day forward, her life was never the same. Guilt and compulsive charity fell away, for she realized that good works must flow from an enlightened self, and not be a shallow substitute for cosmic insight. A million dollars would not persuade Norma to go back to her old, dismal ways.

No man sets aside his old ways to seek the new until he personally feels the need for it. This is why all the great teachers urge men to see the awful condition they are actually in, rather than living by pretty words and non-existent ideals. Talking about love and peace when neither love nor peace is in their hearts is a cunning and destructive evasion of the facts.

What Esotericism Is

Esotericism is a secret science which anyone can learn in order to transform his life amazingly. It provides a new and victorious outlook on life; it gives true and permanent solutions to every problem you may have. It is what Jesus meant by the "bread of life."

HOW THE WAY TURNS CLEAR AND EASY

Most men's minds are like a haunted house, with changing signs out in front to fool the public. The signs sometimes declare it to be a university of wisdom, another time a temple of spiritual peace, another time a merry theater. But the owner of the house knows better, because it haunts him day and night.

All you need to do is to use your basic mental powers *as* powers, and not drain them with worries and fancies and misinformation. As an example of the proper use of mental forces in daily living, take financial affairs. Most people's thinking toward money is tragically faulty. It is a jungle of poor judgment, debts, worries, demands, overspending, carelessness and complaint.

Now, the esoteric way is amazingly clear and simple, yet how few take advantage of it! You need only subject your thoughts toward money to your higher mental forces. This means we need only to think clearly about our financial affairs, and not strike out in the directions mentioned in the preceding paragraph.

When you use your mind correctly, no financial situation, no matter how disastrous from the human viewpoint, can degenerate into a painful personal problem. The financial state is not the difficulty; the human mental state is the only difficulty. Financial problems, like all others, cease to be, when the maker of problems ceases to be the way he is.

An Eastern mystic's teaching reminds us, *"It is our own mind that must be soaked by the rain of truth."*

Imagine a traveler attempting to cross the wide woods at night. He stumbles into a marsh, trips and falls over rocks and vines, all the while frightened and flustered. The next morning he looks back to see that his misery was caused by darkness only. Had he been able to see, his way would have been clear and easy. He wisely decides to travel only during the day. That is an illustration of how psychic darkness causes grief, while esoteric enlightenment makes the way easy.

There is an entirely new way to use your mind. Do not try

to imagine what it is, for it is above imagination. But know that it exists for your new power and true happiness.

HOW TO MAKE MYSTIC SYMBOLISM COME ALIVE

Have you ever noticed how much of your life is mere repetition? Ever notice the habitual dullness? Nothing really changes, does it? Well, you can change all that. You need not live as you do. Take the problem of self-confidence. A confidence based on past victories or on traditional beliefs is no confidence at all. It is like leaning against a crumbling wall built a hundred years ago by careless workmen. An entirely new wall of confidence arises from your use of esoteric materials.

It is valuable practice for you to restate esoteric principles in your own words. Take an idea which has come alive for you and write it down in a single sentence or two, using simple language. *Examples:* (1) *My inner world determines my outer circumstances, so I must concentrate on changing the way I think.* (2) *Self-transformation starts with courageous awareness of myself as I actually am, not as I think I should be.* Use the following space for ideas from this chapter. You will find additional space in Chapter 16.

1. _____

2. _____

3. _____

Raymond H. asked the following questions:

Q. Your books have reduced the great esoteric truths to clear and practical language. I thank you for saving me years of frantic search. Let me ask a question. With all the sermons and books and religions, why is man still in such personal and social chaos?

A. Because what is assumed to be spirituality is not spirituality, but a cunning counterfeit.

Q. Why all this concentration on finding our real nature, instead of working to cure social ills?

A. Because our false nature is the cause of social ills. If your apple tree continually produces sour fruit, does it make sense to endlessly pull them off? Or is the intelligent task to get rid of the tree and replace it with a normal one?

Q. All this seems so serious. Isn't fun a part of life?

A. It is a legitimate feeling to want to have fun, but any activity requiring self-evasion is not fun.

A SPECIAL MESSAGE TO THE READER

What is the condition of man *without* the true guidance of esotericism? Without it, men and women are capable of cruel deceit toward each other. Governments can tyrannize their people and make war against other peoples. And practically everyone, in his egotism, thinks he can be a cure for the sickness, when in fact he is part of the cause.

Since there is no denying man's condition, there is also no denying that *man in fact does not know how to conduct himself on earth for his own best interests.* In spite of all his professions and beliefs and acts, he simply does not know. And what about the famous politicians and intellectuals you see on television who are credited with so much knowledge and experience? They are equally lost. They cry in the night. Their wives know it, but cannot say anything publicly, for they are equally confused and afraid.

Living from esoteric truths is the only way out. Whether this fact is known or accepted or not, it is still a fact.

I want to speak personally to you, the reader, in a very special way for a moment. You must never forget that the esoteric path is always an individual action. It can never be a mass movement, for as the Taoist teacher, Chuang-tse, pointed out, *"Great truths do not take hold of the hearts of the masses."* And this is why, of course, the vast majority of people are unhappy.

You see, mankind is like a party of diners uneasily seated at a table taking part in an absurd drama. The waiters go through the motions of serving food, but actually serve nothing; their hands are empty. Each guest, privately thinking he must be insane, watches to see what the others do. Not wanting to admit participation in a sick situation, everyone goes through the motions of having an enjoyable meal by imitating each other, while covering it up with nervous chatter. They finally depart, tired and hungry.

Everyone is eligible for liberation, but not everyone wants it. Most people prefer pleasurable sensations, which they mistakenly call happiness, but which leave them empty and afraid. However, for you to glimpse the truth of this is a step toward permanent happiness of the cosmic kind. We are becoming truly wise when we detect the hidden pain in what is commonly called pleasure. Up to now, it hasn't been much of a meal, has it?

So do not expect most of your relatives or friends to share your interest in esotericism. They will not do so. It makes no difference. Talk with them about everyday matters, but speak about these things only with those who show persistent interest. You can help each other.

THE THREE SUPREME STEPS FOR CHANGING YOUR LIFE

Step 1: We Must Deeply See the Need for Self-Transformation

Simply defined, self-change means to no longer think, feel, act, desire, respond and live in your usual ways. In what ways do you now live your day? *That* must be changed. Self-transformation has nothing to do with the behavior of others toward you; it means you react with calm self-command to their behavior— whatever it may be.

The need for change must be felt deeply, powerfully. A man must be utterly weary with the stage performance which has been his crushing compulsion up to now. He must be possessed by a strong and persistent urge to understand what is presently a painful puzzle to him. I want to emphasize that his distress must be almost unbearable for true change to open before him. *Everyone* is distressed, but most try to escape it with petty exterior changes.

Therefore, the worse the state a person finds himself in, the greater his opportunity for shattering forever his miserable existence, and replacing it with the bright life. His very crisis is his great chance to cease to live in the mass misery of the world.

Sincerity in seeking the light often comes when a man's personal disaster is so overwhelming, so agonizing, that with a crying leap into the dark, he dares to depart from his former egotisms and superstitions. From that point on, he is on his way up and out.

There was once a man who religiously worshipped the sun, and who spent his days trying to persuade others to do likewise. A series of misfortunes swept away money, health, family. His friends asked, "Why don't you pray to the sun?" The man wearily replied, "What a foolish suggestion!"

How our pious pretenses fall apart when hit by reality! The shattering of illusions can help us see the need for authentic inner change. Though painful at first, it is our true healing. If we would listen to our secret despair, instead of vainly trying to block it out with invented activities, it would tell us everything we need to know. If you understood what it means to admit everything about yourself needing admission, you would know what it means to be a supremely happy human being.

Have you ever noticed the pleasure you feel when finally discarding some junk that has been cluttering your home? Freedom from the accumulated junk of life can give you the same feeling. This is why self-change is everything. If you do not change into something different from what you are, how can you expect your heartache or helplessness to be any different?

We will have the happiness of the truth when we want it more than we want health, popularity, youthfulness, a slender figure, approval from others, or anything else.

"Truth above all, even when it upsets and overwhelms us!" (Henri Frederic Amiel)

Your first correct step: *Deeply see the need for inner change.*

Step 2: We Must See Ourselves As We Actually Are

Having decided to discover a new self, a man must now proceed to the second step with all the persistence and self-honesty he can find. He must explore within himself to see his nature as it actually is, which will be quite different from what he assumed. This calls for courage, for he will be confronted with dozens of negative traits which he will not want to see. For example, his self-observation reveals how often he says one thing in public, but privately thinks the exact opposite. He must not condemn himself for what he sees; he must only quietly and alertly watch them pass across the stage of his mind.

This leads to the surprising discovery that he has been living in all sorts of imaginary ideas about himself. His life has been a collection of idealistic self-pictures, quite flattering to the ego, but out of line with reality.

Why is this process of self-investigation so essential? Because it shows us that we are not as happy or free as we thought. A prisoner under the illusion that his jail cell is his living room will obviously not try to free himself. He must first be aware of his imprisonment, after which he can intelligently plan his escape.

The shock of seeing ourselves as we actually are, and not as we idealize ourselves, is true mental health in action. The entire path to self-liberty can be summed up in just eight words: *Face the things you don't want to face.* By honestly observing our true motives for doing what we do, and not shying away from them, healthy psychic sunshine warms our entire system.

An Example of Necessary Procedure in the Inner Life

Lloyd R. related the following experience: "One evening, while watering the trees in my yard, I noticed that the water pressure was below usual. Wondering whether the other faucets were draining force from my faucet, I checked them out, but found them turned off. I considered several reasons for the low pressure, but came up with nothing definite. Finally, by personal experimentation, I found the simple answer in the very faucet I was using. I had neglected to turn it on full force, as I usually did."

Lloyd continued, "That seems to be a good example of necessary procedure in the inner life. First, we must become aware of whatever is wrong. Then, we eliminate wrong answers. Next, by personal experimenation, we discover the faultiness to be somewhere within ourselves. *Finally, our very discovery shows us how to make correction.*"

Self-freedom Means Self-effort

Self-freedom is a result of self-effort. Society, while seeming to offer help, can only make things worse. The masses are always wrong in their systems for personal deliverance. Only an *individual* can be right. You can live with society, yet not share its psychic darkness. If you don't want to be nipped by the wolf-pack, you must stop running with it. This means you must first observe and then dissolve the wolf-like nature in yourself. Like attracts like, so when you no longer possess a wolf-like nature, the wolves will leave you alone.

Your second correct step: *See yourself as you presently are.*

Step 3: We Must Work Earnestly with Esoteric Principles

We are entering into the greatest adventure on earth!

This book has been prepared to present the great esoteric truths in a simple, clear and practical manner. The aim is to acquaint you with *something that really works to change and enrich your life.* So let's now cover certain procedures which make this personally possible.

An inquirer from Colorado told me, "I am starting all over again." By this he meant that the introduction of esoteric principles had opened his eyes to new ways of handling daily difficulties. That is what we must do—start all over again, with fresh and energetic inquiry. We must begin with an open mind, just as if we were looking at the processes of life for the first time.

"Netti netti" is the Eastern mystic method, meaning, "Not this, not that." Its method consists in finding what is right by first detecting and discarding all that is *not* right. And it is very simple to detect wrongness, if we really wish to do so. Anything causing distress is a false part of us. It is like detecting a wrong note when playing a piano, for that very detection leads to correction.

Don't be faithful to your acquired ideas merely because they are familiar, or because someone else says they are right. "A *pious fiction is still a fiction.*" (Henri Frederic Amiel) Your loyalty belongs to what is right for you, personally. Remember, anything that has not been discovered by your own intelligent effort has not been discovered at all. *"Dare only to believe in yourselves. . . ."* (Friedrich Nietzsche)

Mankind is in trouble because it sees things as they appear to be, not as they are. On this destructive human level, the bad must be made to appear as the good, while the good must be made to appear as the bad. Your aim is total self-transformation by seeing things as they really are. Your goal is to awaken to an entirely new sense of life.

The *Gulistan* tells of a traveler in the desert of Mekkah who grew weary with the long journey. Lying down by the road, he told the camel driver to leave him alone. The driver replied, "Ahead of you is fortune; behind is a band of robbers. If you proceed, all will be well with you; but if you sleep, tragedy."

If a man asks why he should be interested in all these things, the answer is simple enough: Psychic darkness is dangerous.

But to those who are tired of their old ways, there is new hope and brightness just ahead. The majestic mystery can be solved by you. So give attention to, and treasure above all else, the unseen world.

Your third correct step: *Earnestly study esoteric ideas.*

HOW TRANSCENDENT FORCES CAN SUCCEED FOR YOU

Paul N., a businessman, had arrived at that great state where he either had to find the way out or lose his mind. This is a great state? Of course it is. Almost everyone feels at times a sense of mental doom, but Paul was intelligent about it. Recognizing his condition, he used it as his first solid step toward a new and healthy mind. The following ideas helped him along.

Esoteric principles can succeed for everyone, regardless of religious background, feelings of inferiority, past failures, age, and in spite of feelings of guilt and a belief in one's own badness. All these have absolutely nothing to do with it. If you are deep down in a dark well, and look up, you can still see the stars. For instance, a California businessman who freed himself from alcoholism, now uses esoteric principles to aid others in their quest for wholeness.

In order to liberate us toward new happiness, a cosmic truth must fall on our understanding, not on our usual mind. So, the first few times you hear a truth, it may not penetrate to your deeper mind. Therefore, there is no need for discouragement over lack of insight. Just prepare the ground with welcoming attitudes, and the blossoms of realization will appear by themselves.

Also, feel no dismay over your occasional reluctance to practice esoteric principles. No human being who ever found the golden gate ever started with full consent. There are, as you already know, many high walls of resistance, like doubt and inconsistency. Never mind, just do what you can do and keep walking.

Here are helpful answers to questions asked by one of my students:

Q. In spite of all my studies, I still don't know what to do or how to do it. Can you suggest something?

A. Try to see the need for drastic self-transformation. This comes as you perceive with deep feeling the deplorable state you are actually in. The very seeing of your dangerous position awakens healthy action.

Q. I've been told I have a flighty mind, which I'd like to correct for the sake of both my business and my home. What esoteric principle will help?

A. Keep your mind where your body is. While typing a letter or eating lunch, be aware of yourself doing them. Start this practice by awareness of your mental restlessness. For example, your body may be walking a street of New York, while your mind has wandered to an incident in Paris, ten years ago. Constantly bring your mind back to here and now.

Q. How can I reflect upon these things while nagged by a noisy world?

A. By seeing that solitude exists in the mind, not in a physical location.

VALUABLE IDEAS FROM CHAPTER 1

1. Life-healing is possible for all who truly want it.
2. Esoteric wisdom provides genuine life-transformation.
3. The way becomes clear with sincere self-study.

4. You can use your mind in a totally new way.
5. *Let* these esoteric ideas come alive for you.
6. Your personal effort delivers personal enrichment.
7. Deeply see the need for immediate self-change. ⁓
8. Discover your present inward condition.
9. Practice with esoteric principles every day.
10. Realize that esotericism can succeed wondrously for you.

2

The One Way
to Change Your Life
Amazingly

Let's suppose that you are really tired of your life as it is. You have tried everything in order to change, but nothing works. You want very much to get to the heart of things and so change your life.

You are faced with a challenge. Where will you start? How can you tell whether a certain advisor or book is truly accurate? What if the teacher or book is just as confused as you, while cleverly concealing it? What will you do?

There is a way out of this problem, which we can illustrate. Suppose you are an expert at something, perhaps the gem business. You know all about the cutting and polishing of diamonds, rubies, emeralds. One day you meet a man who also claims to be a gem expert. That man needs to talk for only a few minutes before you know the truth about him. How do you know? Because *you* are an expert. His words either match or fail to match what you internally know to be true.

But suppose you knew nothing about gems? There would be no way to judge the man's honesty. If he is a charlatan, he might persuade you with clever words and a confident manner, but in that case you have consented to the deception, for nothing within you backs up his claim.

Where does this leave the sincere seeker? With no problem at all. He must resolutely accept nothing from another that he, in his essential nature, does not accept as true. He must not accept another man's truth; it must be his very own. *He already has at least a grain of truth within himself which can be nourished with honest intentions.* So little by little he will be able to separate the fakers from the true teachers.

This mental clearness is reached by placing the desire for Truth before the desire to lean upon another.

THE PERFECT CURE FOR DAILY DIFFICULTIES

I wonder if you, the reader, are beginning to see something quite wonderful about the esoteric approach? I wonder if you see that no matter what the pain or problem, it can be changed? Esoteric understanding is the perfect cure for whatever is wrong. It turns darkness to light, confusion to clearness, weariness to rest. The following case history proves the point.

How Loretta Overcame Her Destructive Complexes

"I think it best," Loretta S. opened the conversation with me, "that I speak about a specific situation which must be changed. I see the futility of going along with it any more. You have already done that much for me. To get to the point, I feel as if I am not living my own life."

"In what way?" I asked.

She laughed lightly. "I hope it doesn't sound as if I have a persecution complex, but I feel as if everything I do is compulsive. I feel as if I'm being dragged over rocky ground, but have no will to escape. Am I making sense?"

Of course Loretta was making sense. Honesty always makes sense. To be honest about misery is the first necessary step toward removal. Loretta's feeling is common to those who have not as yet found the way out. It is the feeling of being oppressed, of living in a hostile world with no defense, of being at the mercy of unexpected blows from lurking assailants.

But all this can be overcome. I assure you of this. You can be fully in the world and yet removed from its griefs, much like a bottle dancing freely and undisturbed in a stormy sea. All you really need at the start is an intense longing to *find out.*

Loretta had that longing. So together we worked out definite plans for reclaiming her life. The following plan which worked for her can also work for you. Your objective is to *watch.*

Watch the things you do because you assume that you enjoy them. Watch closely and you may make a startling discovery: You don't do them because you really want to, but because you fear *not* to do them. In other words, try to discern your inner compulsion for doing things which only *seem* pleasurable. Are you doing them from a false sense of duty, or from fear of missing out on something, or from nervous habit? Try to find out. Your very awareness melts the psychological chains.

One of Loretta's self-discoveries shook her like an earthquake. She realized that she really did not want to go around helping people after all. She did so compulsively, because she thought it a sign of "goodness." But she finally saw that compulsive "goodness" was only self-flattering egotism. She told me, "You know, I actually resented my so-called generosity."

THE COUNTERFEIT AND THE REAL

No one living by this counterfeit morality is living his own life. He must forget this kind of "charity." It is a great barrier to good essence, because a man mistakes it for interior morality. Anyone, anyone at all can perform exterior acts that may aid others, but they change nothing within the heart of the doer, in fact, they often deepen egotism. Watch the face of someone who performs a public act of charity and you may hear him boast, "See how nice I am!" True good works must spring from good essence. That is why the true teachers insist upon heart-transformation *first.*

We would accept counterfeit money only if unaware that it was counterfeit. If we cannot tell the difference between the real and the imitation, we pay the price. The work of awareness is to show us the difference in psychic matters. It calls for extreme alertness, for the counterfeit is quite clever in masquerading as authentic, as this list explains.

The Counterfeit	The Real
Suppressed anxiety	Inner calmness
Social reform	Personal transformation
Talking about insight	Possessing insight
Conditioned thinking	Clear awareness
Excitement	Contentment
Yesterday and tomorrow	The present moment
Self-hypnosis	Self-enlightenment
Exterior good works	Goodness of essence
Satisfaction of craving	Absence of craving
Mechanical activity	Spontaneous living

Man is the unconscious and unwilling slave of his own wrongness. He prefers the counterfeit to the real, and pays the price. You can stop paying.

It is the simplest task on earth to tell the difference between a true principle and its counterfeit. A principle which really works expresses itself in insight, sanity, balance, control and happiness. A principle which really works *really works.*

So it is worth every ounce of energy and persistence you can spend. Why? Why, because you are getting the most valuable product in heaven and earth—the Truth which sets you free.

HOW YOU CAN ALWAYS LIVE IN BEAUTIFUL WEATHER

Picture a man in his home during a severe storm. Because it makes him nervous, he tries to distract himself with one hasty activity after another. He works at his desk on a business matter, then rushes over to tensely watch television, then hastily gulps his dinner. His sole aim is to escape awareness of the storm that shakes and rattles his house. When the wind breaks a window, he stuffs a rag into the opening; when a tree crashes onto the roof, he drowns out the roar by turning up the television sound.

Now, is this man either happy or intelligent? Obviously not. He is really quite foolish. By trying to make his mind a blank, he not only suffers, but blocks out all possibility of escaping the impending disaster.

You see the parallel here. This is exactly how the vast majority of human beings spend their day. Few will pause in their unthinking rush through life to become aware of their inner storms. But you, if you wish, can be different. You can stop trying to block out the storm, which is an impossibility. But you can get away from it altogether, which is quite a different matter.

It begins with self-examination. Such examination opens the psychic home to beautiful weather.

Here is a question and answer session with Jean B.:

Q. Over and over you stress the need for seeing what is wrong with us. Why not look at what is right?

A. Firstly, because there is nothing right. Secondly, it is the wrongness that makes unhappiness. A doctor needs to discover what is wrong with a patient.

Q. Sometimes I feel like screaming.

A. Of course you do, but because you imitate phony social smiles, you repress the scream behind them. By suppression you lose the shocking insight you could have with an honest scream. The scream itself has no value, but its shock could reveal your panic, previously covered by public smiles.

Q. I am terribly lonely.

A. Loneliness exists when yesterday competes with today and today loses. Live today.

HOW TO BE YOURSELF AND HAPPILY SO

The reason you must be exactly what you are is because there is simply no alternative to it. How can *anything* be other than exactly what it is? Can a green branch be a heavy wheel? A man is only what he is at any given moment, but this changes swiftly; for example, he is sad or elated or puzzled, in turn.

But because man has the capacity for self-delusion, he pretends that he is different from what he is. He does this because he believes there is some benefit in acting out a role, but the opposite is true. His stage performance splits him in two, causing painful self-contradiction.

What is the matter with being who you are and what you are? A man will instinctively remark, "But my badness must be hidden from others; I must put on a good public appearance to hide my badness."

No, he is not even bad, as he supposes, to say nothing of being good. He is neither, for in truth, his essence is the true Good, which is above the human opposites of good and bad. His self-centered labeling of himself as either good or bad must go.

To make all this practical, you must watch the thoughts and feelings which parade through you, but not say "I" to them. You must not identify yourself as being good, bad, right, wrong, or anything else. This impersonal watchfulness breaks the destructive habit of false labeling, and sets you free.

Try being exactly who you are. At first it shocks, then it heals.

How Sylvia Became Her Real Self for True Happiness

"For many years," Sylvia D. told me, "I was the greatest actress outside of Hollywood. My stage was wherever I met other people. I had an amazing number of roles, each one rehearsed to perfection. When others laughed, I laughed, even if it wasn't funny. When the occasion called for an indignant protest against something, my performance was superb. If the scene required an appearance of altruism and unselfishness, I really impressed people with my generosity. And," Sylvia paused momentarily, "I hated every moment of it. I secretly resented every minute and penny I spent on others. I don't think I need to tell you, Mr. Howard, how much I hated myself for being the phony I was."

Sylvia had taken the first honest step toward a new life. Though there was much work to be done, her first glimpse of another way to live provided fresh strength. She learned to drop pretenses. She realized the folly and despair of living from imaginative self-pictures of being generous or righteous or kindly, for she saw how false self-pictures blocked out real self-knowledge.

Sylvia learned to be the only thing it was possible for her to be—herself. And that, she realized with increasing pleasure, was all she really needed for a happy day.

THE ONE WAY TO CHANGE YOUR LIFE AMAZINGLY

The one way to change your life amazingly is to understand fully what it means to be an "aware" person.

Unawareness is the only problem.
Awareness is the only solution.

There it is. You need look nowhere else, for there is nothing else. Pause and ponder.

You can use any other term you like for awareness. You can call it understanding, insight, seeing things as they are, wakefulness, solid sense, freedom from conditioned thinking.

Of what must we become aware? Of what is going on inside us every moment. Suppose you are anxious over the outcome of an important event. Your first and only attention must be to your anxious state, not to the outcome. Though you may not see it as yet, the problem is your anxiety, not the outcome. Attention to outcome perpetuates slavery to anxiety, even when the eventual result matches your original desire. Awareness of anxiety dissolves it, for anxiety is a bluff which you must see through.

Have you noticed that whenever you are desireless toward an event that it has no power to affect you? Watch it. Where there is neither hope nor fear, the result leaves you alone with peace. Do you remember how you once suffered over losing that person who was once in your life? Now that it is over, now that your desire is gone, where is the pain?

There Is No Substitute for Awareness

There is no substitute for awareness, though your friends waste their lives trying to find one. Exterior substitutes and replacements cannot change the heart; everything remains as bad as it was before. Change of religion or residence or spouse changes nothing; the puppets merely dance to a new tune.

You are aware when you let life flow freely, without ego-resistance. You are unaware when you fight whatever happens.

You are aware when you sense that you really do not know what you are doing. You are unaware when you falsely assume you already know what is going on.

You are aware when you realize that no human being can give you anything of value. You are unaware when you feel that others should give you valuable things.

What about this feeling of being owed things by others? It is a painful part of every unawakened person. He secretly demands, "I am *owed* more success, I have a *right* to more money, others *must* appreciate me." What a pity! Such demands arise from misunderstanding. What really bothers him is the knowledge that his invented-self is powerless to change things according to its frightened demands. The frantic ego-self is trying to prove itself, which can never be done.

We must understand cosmic ways, which change us, free us from hostile demands. Then, when we demand nothing, we have everything; we have true riches which cannot be lost. This is what we finally understand. This is awareness at its best.

YOUR SUPERB STARTING POINT

How can you become a self-aware man or woman? Listen to the collected counsel of wise men of all times and places:

Augustine: *"Return today to your true self."*
John Dewey: *"To heal the split between your public self and your real self, enlighten yourself."*
Erasmus: *"Replace superstitious nonsense with honest intentions."*
George Gurdjieff: *"Remember yourself."*
Boethius: *"When everything is seen right, everything becomes all right."*
Rainer Maria Rilke: *"Live fully in the here and now."*
Chuang-tse: *"The way to peace consists in discovering and harmonizing with the true nature of things."*
Soren Kierkegaard: *"Choose to find your own selfhood."*

There is a superb starting point toward psychic health, which is to have the courage and honesty to see the sickness. *"There is no curing a sick man who believes himself in health."* (Henri Frederic Amiel) This means we must get quite personal, and not distract ourselves by prescribing medicine for others. As Jesus stated, *"Physician, heal yourself."* True courage consists in a persistent perception of our actual state, and not living in a dreamland about ourselves. At all costs, we must tell the truth to ourselves, but, surprisingly, after having done so, we discover that the only thing it cost us was our concealed unhappiness.

The Iceberg of the Mind

Imagine a ship whose passage through a channel is blocked by an iceberg. The ship's gun blasts away at the visible portion of the iceberg. As it falls away, the iceberg rises, exposing new sections, which then are also shattered. With patient action, the entire iceberg is broken up, permitting passage.

The human iceberg is a mind hardened with hidden negativities and suppressed desires. The gun is our alert attention, which can be aimed at those negativities which are most visible to us at the present. With consistent action, we can clear the mind of its hard blocks, permitting passage to true life.

All this is really a wonderful action to behold. Even while suffering from a newly observed hardness, perhaps that of envy or discontent, that *painful observation is the very thawing process itself.*

YOUR PROGRESS ON THE ESOTERIC ROAD TO SUCCESS

If we miss the basic fact that man lives from a false sense of self, we miss all else. But by grasping it, we grasp all else. So what is the fact? The fact is, the average man lives from imaginary ideas about himself. He egotistically pictures himself as being wise, strong, kindly, important, generous, and has dozens of other self-flattering notions. But that is all they are—self-applauding imaginings, having absolutely no relation to reality.

To see this, is the beginning of esoteric wisdom. Can you see this? If you have no false notions to defend, who can offend you? The cutting off of this fictitious self is like cutting the strings of a balloon, permitting it to soar up and away to heights of natural flight.

Let's see how this connects with immortality. A man does not really fear the end of his existence on earth; what frustrates him is the shame and humiliation of seeing that he is not the all-powerful god of life he pretends to be in his frantic daily activities. If we will courageously accept the humiliation of not being the little gods we pretend to be, we are consciously in Oneness with the immortality we had all along.

By continuing your march along the royal road you witness a curious process. You see your "self" steadfastly dissolved by the shocks of reality. In earlier days, before you understood what life was all about, you resisted the blows of daily events, for you wrongly assumed they were out to destroy something of value. But now you know better; you realize that what is being destroyed is the false sense of self that kept you afraid for so many years. With this realization, you quicken your step along the royal road, for you know that beyond your acquired self is that which is not acquired, which always existed, and which was truly good.

Whoever has lost his false sense of self can no longer be touched by misfortune. Having lost all—all that is damaging—what more can be taken from him?

Take this as a profoundly practical rule: *Whatever expands the false sense of self is harmful; whatever reduces it is beneficial.*

A WONDROUS DISCOVERY

How Walter Had His Psychic Awakening

"You have rung the bell," Walter L. told me, "about one thing in my life. It is an amazing revelation. I now see what a slave I have been to my emotions. For a long time I falsely assumed that happiness consisted of strong feelings; of excitements and passions. I even loved my angers and my sufferings. How foolish I have been. As you phrase it, I have been asleep all my life. I want to wake up. I hope there is hope!"

"Of course there is. It is a sign of psychic awakening to glimpse the concealed despair behind surface enjoyments."

"But why do I cling to these strong feelings? I sense their destructiveness, but refuse to let them go."

"Because you fear the new state that lies beyond them. You need have no fear whatsoever. Take that one step forward. The new knowledge which can heal you is just one step beyond your fear of taking that step."

Walter was helped by an exploration of a damaging human state which I call a False Feeling of Life. Defined briefly, a False Feeling of Life is any strong feeling which masquerades as psychic health, but which is actually a barrier to wholeness. It includes the feelings of excitement, passion, pride, power, criticism, depression, malice, terror, envy, accusation, rudeness and the counterfeit versions of love and sympathy.

Notice for yourself how people leap at almost anything—a news item, a casual remark, anything at all—to induce strong feelings in themselves. For instance, one of the worst blows a man could strike against himself is to use another person's tragedy or shame as a source of private excitement, which masquerades as sympathy.

Now, why this frantic desire to lose oneself in strong emotion? Why do most people depend upon it to carry them through their day? *People anxiously seek a False Feeling of Life because it distracts them from their painful emptiness which they fear to face.*

We have here a fantastic tragedy. Human beings treasure a False Feeling of Life which destroys them, because that is all they know. And because this falseness is all they have, they will fight fiercely anyone who tries to take it from them. They fight for their poison!

But there is hope. If we are tired of the game, we can cease to play it. We can courageously face what we have been evading all these years. We can come back to ourselves. We can face the seeming emptiness, thereby calling its bluff, to discover wondrously what is on the other side.

What is on the other side is Real Life.

HOW TO CLAIM YOUR PSYCHIC AWARENESS

Here are answers to vital questions from my lecture audience that undoubtedly will apply to you also.

Q. I feel all alone and forsaken.

A. It is just as impossible for you to be forsaken as it is impossible for wetness to forsake water. Your very nature is Oneness with the Higher Power, but ignorance of this gives false feelings of desolation.

Q. I agree with what you teach, yet nothing changes for me. For example, I realize the folly of living from borrowed opinions, yet my life remains the same.

A. That is because only one horse, that of intellectual agreement, is pulling you toward trueness. Contrary horses, of which you are as yet unaware, pull in the opposite direction. They are the horses of pride, laziness, and so on. Try to be aware of them; otherwise you will experience no desired change.

Q. I like the way you simplify these complex questions, so please tell me, in a few words, the way to true happiness.

A. Simply exist, but not as this or that kind of person. You exist *now*, so what else need you do? Understand this and watch unhappiness fall away.

Hypnotized humanity goes nowhere. The arm-in-arm allies of one war become the enemies of the next war. But you, *as an individual,* can go somewhere. What are the new states of the man with esoteric experience?

Anxiety about losses is replaced with calm understanding. His feelings cannot be hurt by sharp tongues. Business difficulties, no matter how oppressive to others, leave him at ease. No longer does he get entangled with the wrong people, including those of the opposite sex. Because he is no longer hiding anything, he has no worry that others might see through him at any moment. He cheerfully realizes that all problems, when met with quiet insight, fade into nothingness. Because he lives only in the present, fears of the future have no power over him. No longer does he feel like a butterfly caught in the rain.

People look for happiness where it is not, like a man searching for pearls in the desert. Where is the right place to search? William Law explains: *"Begin to search and dig in thine own field for this pearl of eternity . . . and when thou hast found it thou wilt know that all which thou hast sold or given away for it is as mere a nothing as a bubble upon the water."*

IMPORTANT POINTS FROM CHAPTER 2

1. Make the Psychic Truth your very own Personal Truth.
2. Daily difficulties are cured through esotericism.
3. Learn to separate the counterfeit from the real.
4. You can live always in beautiful psychic weather.
5. It is possible and necessary to be yourself.
6. Practice the magic of daily personal awareness.
7. Your mind must be cleared of its hardened ideas.
8. The reduction of the ego-self delivers newness.
9. Abandon a False Feeling of Life.

3

The New Way
to Use Your Powers of
Mind

The Case of a Rich Man in Chaos

Leonard D. telephoned me to say he would like to drop in
to discuss the mysteries of life. He had only a few minutes, he
said, because important business projects kept him hopping. Driving up in an expensive automobile, he stepped briskly out, dressed
in a very fine suit.

Inside, he broke out talking at once, telling me about himself.
He spoke boldly, with frequent and emphatic gestures. He said
that for a long time he had not the slightest notion of what he
was doing here on earth. Then, he happened to attend a meeting where a new and exciting doctrine was taught. He had followed it for the past year, going to meetings and reading their
books. So now, everything was much different for him. He said
the system provided all the answers, among them the secret of
happiness and an assurance of future immortality.

Once, when he paused for breath, I asked whether he was a
personally happy man. He did not seem to hear the question,
but launched into a lengthy speech about the need for human
brotherhood. When I asked whether he was personally free of
anxiety about the future, he told me that his wife was not much
interested in these things, but that was only because she did not
see their importance.

An hour later, in the middle of a sentence, he glanced at his watch, which caused him to jump up to say he had to go. Then, forgetting I was there, he turned slowly away, his eyes dazed and unseeing for a moment. Resuming his quickness, he almost ran to his car and drove away.

I have met Leonard a thousand times. So have you. That may not have been his name, but that is the chaotic condition. The Leonard-nature in anyone needs the real transformation provided by esotericism.

HIDDEN DYNAMIC FACTS ABOUT YOUR MIND

We do not know ourselves until we know our own minds. Self-acquaintance comes by noticing our hidden motives and desires, which will always be quite different from what we assume they are. For example, a man could see that he is motivated by two main desires—to gain pleasure and to avoid pain. By studying his desires, he could understand their ways; he could detect and banish self-defeating ones. He could also see that by permitting another person to think for him, he opens himself to every delusion and disaster of which that person is capable.

Why an Intellectually Conditioned Mind Fails to Protect

The conditioned mind cannot protect against the assaults of life, for it is unknowingly a part of the forces of assault. You might as well appoint a wolf to guard sheep. Why must we insist upon going beyond mere opinions gathered by the intellect? Because the painful questions asked by the heart cannot be answered by a confused mind. Mystic William Blake likened man's limited vision to a prisoner in a cave, who can glimpse only a small part of the world through the narrow cracks in the walls.

As esoteric principles blend with your nature, your mind regains its original sharpness. What happens is really amazing. When confronted by a problem of finances or domestic life or school studies, all its powers come together for peak efficiency. You will see that it is better *to be comfortable with yourself* than to be anything else with other people. You will realize that the less guilty your conscience the less money you may give to charity and the more trueness you will give to the world. Your feelings can no longer be hurt because you are no longer living from feelings which can be hurt.

Cecil H., a student of esotericism, asked me the following questions. My answers can help you also.

> Q. Your insistence upon simple and clear thinking has washed away many nonsensical notions I used to have about the spiritual life. Will you please define clear thinking.
>
> A. It is when you see anything, whether inward or outward, without reacting with either gladness or sadness.
>
> Q. You say that clear awareness of the awful mess we are in can start correction, but how can the mere seeing of something produce benefit?
>
> A. If you are idling in the forest and suddenly see that it is on fire, do you continue to idle there?
>
> Q. I am afraid.
>
> A. Fear is a thought only, but not seeing this, you think you are afraid of something, perhaps a threatening person or a forthcoming crisis. All fear arises from a false sense of self. When wrong ideas about yourself fade away, fear also vanishes.

THE MARVELOUS THIRD WAY OF THINKING SUCCESSFULLY

I want to tell you about an entirely new way to use your mind. I call it *The Third Way of Thinking.* It is one of the most important mental powers presented in this book.

The intellectually conditioned mind thinks in *opposites.* For example, you may think that one candidate for public office is good. That is your *first* way of thinking. But if you think he is good, you must also think of his opponent as bad. That is your *second* way of thinking. Or, you think that being married provides comfort. But that means you must also think that the single state lacks comfort. So an opinion toward anything is the first way of thinking, while its opposite is the second way. Every opinion must have an opposite, just as one end of a stick is opposed by the other end.

Now, do you see the hovering harm in thinking from a fixed viewpoint? *It means you are at the mercy of the opposite, which may take over at any moment.* If a husband insists upon his wife behaving in a certain way, he will be hurt when she behaves differently. If an employee believes himself entitled to a promotion, he will suffer when refused. In other words, a person attaches himself to one end of a situation, then falls into gloom when the opposite appears. The thrill of winning is always paired off with the dread of losing. *This is how the human race lives and agonizes.*

The Third Way of Thinking has no attachments to either end of the stick. It is *above* the opposites. This means it is *above* human opinions, desires, demands, neuroses. In turn, this means that the person using The Third Way of Thinking remains peaceful in spite of all happenings. He cannot be wounded by the defeat of his position because he has none. Being above both loss and gain, he has Supreme Success.

When you employ The Third Way of Thinking you cannot be frightened by anything. Picture two scared men who crouch on opposite sides of a high wall, each thinking himself opposed on the other side by a vicious tiger. But a third man who sits quietly on top of the wall knows very well there is no tiger.

Someone may object, "But where would we be without human opinions?" Let me ask, where are we *with* human opinions? You need only a brief glance at world events to suspect that the psychopathic inmates are in charge of the asylum.

LET YOUR DAY ALWAYS BE AN ADVENTURE

Human opinions are formed by accident and hardened by repetition. We cling to acquired opinions only because they give the illusion of being wise opinions. This creates division and hostility between people. We are like actors in cowboy costumes who believe the role is real, and so we fight with other actors in Indian costumes.

Test it for yourself. How would you feel if suddenly deprived of a strong opinion you now hold? You would feel empty, without a sense of self. But your understanding of that emptiness opens the royal road before you.

How to Start

Here is how to start using The Third Way of Thinking for rich benefits. Meet whatever happens to you without unconsciously comparing it with something else. See it all by itself, with no reference to former things. Have no opinions that it is better or worse than something else. For instance, a retired person might feel purposeless because he no longer has his former activities or prestige. By dropping comparisons between what *was* and what *is*, the present day has its own purpose. Ceasing to compare one thing with another is a valuable exercise in The Third Way of Thinking.

When Jesus taught "Resist not evil" he expressed a profound esoteric truth. This means not to resist what you *call* evil, and you call anything evil which goes contrary to your conditioned desires. To resist such evil implies the existence of a separate self which knows what it is doing and which can solve problems. But no such self exists. What resists evil is a human desire or vanity or arrogance which insists that events should conform to its demands. But if we wisely let reality be whatever it wishes to be, that very surrender destroys insistence and vanity, leaving us at peace.

To understand life truly we must meet it as an unplanned adventure, not with fixed plans which seem to offer security. Suppose a man wanted the adventure of roaming through the woods, but feared what he might meet. Because of this, he walks in his sleep, setting out certain markers to guide him safely through the parts of the woods with which he is already acquainted. The next morning he follows the markers, deceiving himself into thinking it a new adventure into the woods. Such a man cannot discover the new, he can only follow the old. For true discovery, the markers must be ignored, he must plunge boldly into the very woods he fears. In time, he will see that those fears existed only in his false imagination.

HOW MENTAL MIRACLES HAPPEN

Everyone who has ever emerged from the human jungle to enter the new world of sanity has said these three things to himself:

1. I suspect the existence of an entirely new life.
2. Presently, I do not know what it is.
3. With right and persistent search, it can be known.

The Need for a Fresh Mind

Suppose a man is walking home when a ball flies over a fence, striking his head and leaving him dizzy. He continues on his way with dazed mind and step. He suddenly finds himself in front of traffic, barely escaping with his life. Then, surprisingly, he finds himself quarrelling with a screaming woman who has somehow entered his life. Next, he finds himself in the company of a rough gang of people who have violent intentions. Faintly realizing his domination by dizziness, he lurches forward in fear of the next danger.

But as he nears home, his mind gets clearer. He begins to see where he is and what is happening. He realizes why and how he ran into dangers. Finally returning to normal, he walks with ease and with no fear of dangers.

That is all we really need—a fresh mind. But this simple solution is not romantic enough to many people; they prefer glamourous packages over valuable contents. But as mystic Henry Suso points out, *"There is nothing pleasurable save what is uniform with the utmost depths of the divine nature."* To have a *simple, uncomplicated mind* is the same thing as having divine nature.

You can work miracles with a young mind. I will give you a hint of one of them: *If you feel unhappy, but don't mind feeling that way, how would you then feel?*

Here is a sure method for profitable thinking: Notice how your present way of thinking continually attracts unpleasant circumstances, unwanted events, the wrong kind of people. Wrong thinking attracts conditions which are similar to its own nature, just as a shark attracts and is attracted to other sharks.

So what would right thinking attract? Reflect on this.

HOW TO CHANGE UNWANTED CONDITIONS

If we do not use our minds rightly to make our lives right, what *will* we use? To try to end painful conditions by fighting them is endless and useless. We might as well try to push away fog. Ralph Waldo Emerson offers this clue, *"Make circumstance —all circumstance—conform to the law of your mind. Be always a king, and not they, and nothing shall hurt you."*

Unhappiness exists because unawareness exists. Unhappiness is nothing but a state of unawareness. If you were totally aware of a situation which now grieves you, the grief would cease instantaneously. So the only thing you can do or need to do is to awaken from psychic sleep, from unawareness.

Psychic sleep is largely characterized by mental movies. Notice for yourself how agitation is accompanied by an imaginative film running through the mind. The film of a past mistake unreels itself before your mental eyes, sending shudders of pain throughout your system. These mental movies are one type of unawareness, of psychic slumber. If the film is snapped, which can be done through esotericism, the stranglehold of unawareness is also snapped.

A Marital Problem Solved

Laura G. plunged into grief when her husband no longer wanted to live with her. Her state was a painful combination of shock, hurt, panic and bitterness. During the long, sleepless nights, she wept, wondering, "Why should this happen to me?"

Let's put ourselves in Laura's place for a few minutes, to see what she might do, were she armed with esoteric thinking.

To begin, there are definite things she would *not* do. She would not ask her friends for advice, for their secret lives are just as disturbed, though in different areas. She would not race out to latch onto the nearest man, in an effort to replace the lost one, or to prove that someone likes her after all. And, most importantly, she must not surrender to self-pity, to hostility toward the man, and to subtle schemes in order to attract attention, which is pure egotism.

No, the esoteric way is utterly different from all those traps which snare so many. There is no hope for those who insist upon labeling a trap as an exit. But there is hope, the right kind of hope, for those who choose the true esoteric path.

The True Approach Never Fails

Laura wants nothing to do with making matters worse through false solutions. So what does she do? She does something quite unique. *She becomes aware of the total situation,* in this manner:

"Here I am, heartsick and afraid because my husband has left me. What has happened inside me to cause this panic? Well, esotericism says that my grief is caused by my false reaction to the situation. I don't fully understand this, but take it as a starting point for intelligent exploration. It means I must take full self-responsibility for reaching the kind of insight providing freedom; I must not lean on anyone else. I must wake up from my self-induced nightmare; *I must become aware.*

"I think I am on the right track, for I notice how my mind operates toward the situation. It flashes mental movies of the good times we used to have together; the picnics and the dinners, the kisses and bedroom intimacies. All these accumulated experiences gave me a sense of security, of being anchored to something permanently pleasant.

"Now it is all gone. I feel empty, lost, lonely. What is the cause of such pains? I think I understand where I am going wrong. The great mistake is in trying to hold onto yesterday, rather than living fully and freely in the present moment. The problem is my insistence upon comparing yesterday with today. Because my present state is so new and so unknown, I cling fondly to mental movies of past pleasures. But it is the very mental movies which create my distress. Now, if I will live totally in the present, without imaginative films, without attachments to the past, then I would experience the freedom found in the present. When I am one with the present, I am also one with its freedom and happiness."

When troubled by anything whatsoever, we can either surrender to our own destruction or we can surrender to the liberating truth within. When the truth is allowed to come, happiness, freedom and sanity come with it.

HOW TO BREAK THROUGH THE ROADBLOCKS OF LIFE

Here are various roadblocks along the esoteric highway. You can break through them with self-insight.

1. *False assumptions:* If we will suspect that our false assumptions *are* assumptions, and not the facts they seem to be, our days brighten. If we are living in an uneasy truce with life, we have false assumptions.

2. *Searching outside ourselves:* Nothing exterior to us can do it. Zen teaches that salvation is so close we cannot see it, like a man crying for water, while waist deep in a lake.

3. *False hope in the future:* Beware of those who urge you to sacrifice today for some misty heaven tomorrow. It will never come. The right time to wake up is right now.

4. *Self-condemnation:* After making mistakes, self-awareness is the right action, not self-reproach. Self-condemnation only leads you away from the path, while giving the appearance of humility.

5. *Laziness toward self-awakening:* Let shocks and sufferings awaken you, for it means their ending. It is as if you might shake yourself awake while driving the highway, knowing that sleep spells disaster.

6. *Wrong attention:* It is a pointless waste of time and energy to criticize the behavior of others, either openly or secretly. Our task is to study our own mental states and our own behavior.

7. *False belief in a fixed fate:* With his usual bluntness, Arthur Schopenhauer wrote, "*What people commonly call Fate is, as a general rule, nothing but their own stupid and foolish conduct.*" Do not believe that your life is fixed and unchangeable, for all can be altered, magnificently.

8. *Dishonesty:* As long as the ego-self gets a reward from evil, it will lie about it and shamelessly call evil good. The detection of dishonesty is a first step toward true happiness.

9. *Discouragement and depression:* There is no need to be depressed about anything whatsoever. The rainbow is in the sky all right, but we must clear away the overhanging branches to see it.

10. *Compromise:* Do not go half way. There is one declaration which every earnest seeker must make: "I will *not* settle down in my present psychic location."

11. *Vanity and egotism:* Look at that foolish man, boasting of his earthly success. He is like a man running desperately over a collapsing bridge, who stops to call out to his friends to please notice his pretty new jacket.

12. *Dependency:* We cannot become a musician by playing a borrowed phonograph record. But we can become a cosmic artist by listening to the original music within our nature, where there is never a false note.

HOW DREAMS MAY BE MADE TO COME TRUE

Do you notice something interesting about the preceding ideas? Do you see how many of them go against your present concepts? That is good. It means that they can produce the results opposite to those you have been getting.

This is a perfect example of what happens all along the esoteric path. What we formerly took as an enemy, now becomes a friend. What we used to think was the friend, is now seen as uselessness. True, there is a shock involved in changing our viewpoints, but beyond the shock is relief. As Henri Frederic Amiel explains, *"The natural man in us flinches, but the better self submits."*

To grow in happiness we must distinguish between what we *can* do and what we *must not try* to do. We must see that we are not responsible for the cosmic life-movement in itself, but we are responsible for making our lives move in harmony with it. It is similar to an airplane. We need not create the scientific laws governing flight; they exist already. If there are faults in the airplane, making it unable to harmonize with the principles of flight, it is our duty to repair it. Likewise with life. Our task is to correct the faulty mechanism within, which makes psychic flight natural and pleasant.

By working on yourself correctly, your dreams come true. But these fulfilled dreams are not those envisaged by your surface character, but by your essence. Your essence hints at what could be true, then asks if you are willing to shed illusions in order to attain them. By replying in the affirmative, your dreams come true.

How a Businessman Won Success

The ideas you have just read are wonderfully practical. They work for you in the way you want things to work. Herbert M. came to tell me about the success he had won since applying them to his daily life.

He said, "I was skeptical when you said that my only problem was the misuse of my mind. As you recall, I told you about my business life, which set me squarely between my employers and the public. I got blame and criticism from both sides, which made me nervous and irritable. You told me to try to see that the criticisms were striking against my false sense of self, which always gets nervous and upset when under attack.

"Well," Herbert continued, "I see what you mean. If there is no false self to feel the attacks, they pass almost unnoticed. So I am putting an end to my ego-self. I understand that no harm is external; I can only harm myself with wrong reactions. I am really surprised by all this—how could I have been so asleep? But thanks."

HOW GRIEF CAN VANISH IN A FLASH

The following exchange of thoughts with an audience took place at one of my lectures:

Q. If the truth seeks to make itself heard, why don't we hear it?

A. Because it responds only to sincere human request. To phrase it differently, if you want to hear the music from your record player, you must first shut off your vacuum cleaner.

Q. I wish I could grasp one particular point you make. You say we are free from something only when we cease to think about it. Yet, we must think things out.

A. If your shoes are too tight, you are forced to think about your cramped feet. In perceiving the discomfort, you know something is wrong, causing intelligent action which makes correction. Once correction is made, you need no longer think about it. You *think* about pain, but have no need to think about happiness.

Q. All the classic teachings agree upon the need for self-surrender, but to whom or what do I surrender?

A. To your true nature within.

The Importance of the Cosmic Command, "Be Still"

Have you ever quietly observed a conversation between two of your friends? You know what I mean. One of them tries to tell of an adventure, but the other repeatedly interrupts with exclamations or breaks in with a similar experience of his own. Unfortunately, that is how most people listen—or fail to listen—to the greatest adventure story of the ages. Instead of quiet receptivity to the cosmic story, the mind and mouth nervously pop up with self-references or rejections.

Our own silence tells us the marvelous story. The whole of esotericism is contained in the biblical advice: *"Be still."*

There is a happy way of life which is not manufactured by the mind's desires or imaginations. It is above human inventions. We can have it, but we need not demand it. If we could only see, it would be there, just as the sun is there without demand.

Change your thinking and you change your world.

You could be sitting all alone in your room, in anguish, regretful over the past, anxious in the present, and worried about the future, having nothing, hopeful for nothing—and if you would snap the hypnosis of your mind, all grief would vanish in a flash.

IMPORTANT POINTS IN CHAPTER 3

1. Become acquainted with the powers of your mind.
2. Practice the marvelous Third Way of Thinking.

3. Replace human opinions with esoteric facts.
4. Make every day a new adventure in self-discovery.
5. A young and fresh mind can work miracles.
6. You can certainly change all unwanted conditions.
7. Esotericism provides a unique kind of life-victory.
8. With persistent esoteric self-work, your dreams always come true.
9. With right thought griefs can vanish in a flash.
10. Use this chapter's ideas to crash through barriers.

4

How Mystic and Cosmic Principles Supply Refreshing Days

If the principles by which you now live do not free you of secret despair, they are worthless. If they do not abolish the need for frantic pursuits of happiness, it is wise to get new principles.

There is true conquest and there is false conquest. False victory is like a dictator who marches over a neighboring country, but finds himself a captive of the very people he has supposedly beaten. They snipe at his soldiers, steal supplies, and make his occupation generally miserable. Do you see the parallel here? How many men are slaves of a successful business? How many women are dragged down by a marriage which appears so victorious in public?

The fact is, Truth has already won the battle for us, but each person must accept the accomplished cosmic victory, and not vainly insist upon being the bemedaled general or colonel, with his name in the papers. True conquest is over ourselves, with no public honors.

Do not think that cosmic principles are beyond your understanding. Esoterically, you *are* these principles, just as a rose includes all the powers of the flower kingdom. The truth is not outside you, so you need not try to create anything at all; you need only *reveal* what you already are. Simplify your thinking toward cosmic principles by seeing them as healings for our split nature. Here are ten healings for your personal application:

1. The inner determines the outer.
2. Let self-confusion lead you to self-work.
3. Fear is the product of truth refused.
4. Awareness is everything.
5. Desire no gratifications or rewards from anyone.
6. Things go right when the mind goes right.
7. Go deeper; much deeper.
8. Do not fear to be all alone in your search.
9. You need only come home to yourself.
10. When we are ready, so is the Answer.

HOW ONE MAN BANISHED NERVOUSNESS

"I can't even state my problem very clearly," said Marvin K., a businessman, "except to say I'd like more self-confidence. Can the laws you speak about help me?"

"We can start," I told him, "with a basic principle. Do not try to add what you think is good, but seek to subtract what you sense is wrong."

"I guess you mean my aim must be to abolish nervousness."

"Yes, because your nervousness has a false foundation in your lack of knowledge."

We discussed some fundamental ideas as follows: Nervousness occurs whenever we want something of a psychological nature. Our arising desire starts the shaking process because we fear we won't get it or that it might fail us after awhile. For example, if I wish to impress or influence you in any way at all, I must unlawfully appeal to your hopes and desires. My own unnaturalness punishes me on the spot with nervousness. Plotinus stated that whoever violates natural laws will feel it at once in a loss of natural happiness.

"But," Marvin objected, "how can we stop wanting things from other people? In my business I want efficiency from my employees and sales from my customers."

"Please listen carefully. It is of utmost importance for you to grasp this. If you do not use your business for ego-expansion, it will never be a problem to you, regardless of sales or no sales. Your only motive for working must be to earn your daily bread, *never for self-gratification*. Millions of businessmen live with jangled nerves and fearful frustrations because they do not see this simple fact. But you, by persisting until you understand, will not only be a happy businessman, but a far more competent one. You won't waste your energies in depression and irritation."

Marvin thoughtfully listened as we connected this principle with others, like these: Calmness appears when we have set aside the invented self, which is always trying to prove itself—in vain. In other words, nervousness occurs when falseness parades around as essence. So all we really need is self-discovery, and self-discovery comes with voluntary self-shattering.

Businessmen reading this book can prove all this for themselves at the office. Others can apply it to their own areas, including the home.

THE SHOCKING TRUTH ABOUT HUMAN AND COSMIC LAWS

Man-made laws cannot change or purify a man. Only esoteric principles can do that. Human codes can only punish exterior offenses. Their only influence over inner badness is to suppress it, to make one fearful of the consequences of public misconduct. This is why Jesus and other true teachers taught change of heart, rather than exterior reform.

Human laws cannot enforce cosmic principles, nor do human lawmakers want them. They fear self-exposure from cosmic codes. There is a cosmic law against hypocrisy, but if a human one existed, everyone would have to rush out and arrest everyone else.

The only human codes which are right are those based in universal morals. For example, it is against human law to physically attack another person. The man who does so, may or may not be caught and punished by the court, but he is always punished on the spot by himself, whether aware of it or not. We may escape human laws, but never the laws of our own nature.

Unenlightened men are behind laws which attempt to level men down to mediocrity and uniformity. They hope to stifle the spiritual purity which appears here and there in various men, and which threatens their false claims to authority. Also, if you put the same costume on all the actors, who can pick out the villains?

The greater number of human laws in a nation, the less it lives from esoteric principles. Neither knowing nor wanting cosmic legislation, human beings frantically invent their own substitutes, which turn out to be decorated traps. *"Distrust all those who talk much of their justice!"* (Friedrich Nietzsche)

Human leadership is summed up in an anecdote from the *Gulistan,* a book of Persian wisdom. A cruel king asked a spiritual teacher, "What is the best kind of worship?" With rare courage, the teacher replied, "For you, it is to sleep half the day. In that way you will not harm so many people."

A student of the esoteric way need not be infected by the sickness of society's hypocritical moralities. He can remain personally healthy by seeing that no human agency has anything of value for his inner self. Nothing is above the Truth.

When living in harmony with universal laws, we are free of the pressure of foolish human laws. *Anything understood on the cosmic level cannot mentally bind you on the human level.* Jesus told Peter to take a coin from the mouth of a fish and pay his taxes. Jesus was above human laws of taxes, but paid them to prevent animal-like accusations which painfully punish the very accusers. That is true love.

As we will see in Chapter 5, there is a sure way to detect an artificial law. It must always include a *threat.* Though presented in a subtle manner, it makes it perfectly clear as to what will happen to you if you fail to agree, conform, follow, pay, believe. Such threats are immoral, and should be seen as such.

Cosmic laws never threaten; they quietly invite.

HOW TO LET COSMIC POWERS WORK FOR YOU

Suppose you are walking down the avenue to keep an 8 P.M. appointment. Your watch is out of order, so you look into several shop windows for the right time. Strangely, all the clocks give a different time, so you don't know whether to hurry or slow down.

However, you take the word of one of the clocks which appears authoritative. But upon reaching your destination, you find that all the clocks were wrong, due to a power failure in town.

So it is with us. If we are in conflict of any kind, we can be sure we are entertaining a fancy of some kind. Only the entrance of esoteric fact can chase it out. Let's take a single area and see how man's ignorance and violation of cosmic law confuses his appointment with his own goodness. I select that unhealthy need to dominate people and events.

In a vain attempt to perpetuate the illusion of power, the ego-self frantically interferes with and tries to shape exterior events. But since the ego-self is an illusion itself, it has no power to do anything. Cosmically, everything happens the way it must happen. The ego-self is frustrated and angered when results differ from its demands, and is puffed up with pride when results happen to coincide with its wishes. To be free of the whole mess, we must see through this illusion of self. This is where esoteric wisdom enters.

When welcomed, nothing can prevent cosmic laws from working for you. You might as well try to stop the wind from blowing; it is that natural. This point led to these questions:

Q. I would like to enjoy this effortless life of which you speak, but need to know how to start.

A. Go through the next few hours with an absence of your usual sense of self. Do not believe that *you* are doing anything; see everything as simply happening to you, all by itself. Feel yourself guided by something other than your own thoughts and decisions. Do not try to identify who or what is guiding you; quietly follow. After awhile, a sense of something totally different will enter.

Q. In what way?

A. One surprise will be much less anxiety than you had expected. You see, as we abandon a false sense of self, it frightens us, for we know no other guide. But with persistence in seeing yourself as a follower, not as a doer, the strangeness fades away, to be replaced by refreshing confidence.

Q. Does this experience change my exterior behavior?

A. Certainly, and in a healthy way, for cosmic force is now

expressing itself through you. It expresses itself in happiness, sanity, decency and all else truly good.

HOW RICHARD TURNED CRUELTY INTO KINDNESS

We learn the truth about the great cosmic universe as we first learn the truth about ourselves. If you become acquainted with your own home, you can go on to explore your neighborhood, then the town, nation, world, and outer space. You understand how one affects the other. With this knowledge you deal intelligently with each area; you know exactly how to think toward events, your health, sex, career, and so on. Your knowledge is like a cheery fire which warms and brightens everything in a room. It includes your contacts with other people, for esotericism makes you an expert in human relations.

There is pure magic in such insight. The experience of Richard A. is excellent evidence. A former friend dealt him a cruel blow, creating chaos in both his business and domestic life. Coming as it did after many years of what he thought was a close friendship, the treachery was a sharp shock. It almost shook him to pieces, Richard admitted. But he was an unusual man when it came to blows from life, for he was deeply interested in esoteric enlightenment.

Richard went to work. First, he quietly surveyed the entire happening. He noticed how deeply he had been mentally wounded, which made him aware that this reaction was all wrong because it was self-damaging. This led to insight concerning his unrealistic expectations from others. He saw that people must behave according to the way they actually are, not in the way he expected or preferred. In other words, he must let things happen as they must happen.

This was already great gain, but the best was yet to come. His deepening insight showed him that the only problem in the whole wide world was his negative reaction. And this negative reaction resulted from lack of understanding about himself and others. Now he knew exactly what to do. *He must let this seeming betrayal fall on his clear understanding, not on the ego-self, which always gets hurt and upset when things turn out contrary to expectations.*

Richard reported, "That seeming cruelty, though a shock at the time, turned out to be a great kindness. It helped me to sweep out at least a dozen false reactions to life, which had kept me an unconscious slave."

THREE EXTRAORDINARY PRINCIPLES FOR SELF-ENRICHMENT

1. *The Principle of Material Use:* Material items which come your way may be used legitimately for comfort and convenience, but must not be used for ego-gratification.

The Application: Form no psychological attachments to material things, but give attention to the invisible world of true values.

The Enrichment: Freedom from competitive acquisition, liberty from fear of loss, the ability to enjoy everything, while tied to nothing.

2. *The Principle of Spontaneity:* Freshness and spontaneity flow out from us as we submit all our various parts to cosmic power.

The Application: Through alert self-observation, be aware of the contradictory tyrants within, that pull you this way and that.

The Enrichment: Spontaneity, pleasantness, with no painful self-contradictions.

3. *The Principle of Progress Through Pain:* All forms of heartache and grief can be used to attain true happiness.

The Application: Do not resist nor resent nor evade pain, but quietly study its nature.

The Enrichment: The falling away of unhappiness, and the appearance of dynamic living.

If you fail to develop your ability to recognize a diamond when you see one, you will walk right past dozens of diamonds, never knowing what you missed and what could have been yours. You will receive cosmic riches as soon as you recognize them as such. Recognition is everything.

Where does this recognition start? Within yourself. Cosmic treasures exist both within you and outside, but start your detective work inside the very self you now occupy. You are not only a collection point for all cosmic power; you *are* that which you think you must obtain. Henri Frederic Amiel penetrated this secret when he wrote: *"To become divine then is the aim of life: then only can truth be said to be ours beyond the possibility of loss, because it is no longer outside us, nor even in us, but we are it, and it is we; we ourselves are a truth. . . ."*

Have you ever noticed that when you finally see something clearly that you dimly *suspected* it all along? This proves the abiding existence of truth within, but we are so fearful of our own deliverance!

HOW TO CONQUER YOUR DESTRUCTIVE, NEGATIVE EMOTIONS

Obviously, a man who has no interest in asking a question, will not receive an answer. But any man who sincerely and persistently asks what his life is all about, will not be denied the answer.

With this confidence, we can profitably ask questions regarding those unhappy states within a human being called negative emotions. A clear grasp of the principles surrounding negative feelings is certain to begin the rescue.

Few things are more senseless or damaging than false feelings. Just as weeds choke out a colorful garden, so do wrong emotions spoil our day. Take this example. A man's psychic level instantly signals itself to others, telling them how to treat him. Now, suppose a man is loaded with various negativities, including timidity and doubt. Others easily detect them, *for they show in whatever the man does or says.* Unfortunately, when people detect weakness in another, they tend to attack him, to take advantage of him, for it reminds them of their own disliked weakness. So this weak man helplessly falls victim because he does not understand himself.

Almost everyone with whom I talk wishes to find relief from a burdened self. Often, I bring up these points about negative emotions which we are now covering. These feelings must be recognized, admitted, understood. That is how life eases itself. So think of each new esoteric insight on your part as a *new relief.*

To cease falling a victim to our own false feelings we must be shocked by what they do to us. The greater the awakening shock the better. It does no good to sadly deplore human jealousy or cruelty. A man must get personal; he must be stunned at what they do to *him*. *He must never forget that negative emotions:* (1) Cause personal and social misery, (2) waste life's energy, (3) distract him from his quest of wholeness, (4) supply a False Feeling of Life, (5) prevent pleasant human relations, (6) harm physical health, and (7) keep him confused and exhausted.

You can be sure of one thing. Beyond the false sense of power provided by deceitful emotions, there is true power. Eastern mystics describe it as daring to enter the dragon's cave where the shining jewels are hidden. Carefully consider the following: If our first move is to find good in ourselves, that seeming good will be bad disguised as good, a mere product of vanity and imagination. But if we first see the bad, without reacting to it, we come to the true good. True good is above human labelings of good or bad. It is not the product of passing human egotism, but is enduring cosmic goodness.

How Emotional Energy Was Saved for Useful Work

I discussed these principles with Steve L. He showed a special interest in ways to save his emotional energy for useful work. He asked, "Is there a practical experiment I can use in daily affairs? I want to work with myself down at the office."

I told him, "When someone asks you a question about anything at all, try to answer as briefly and directly as possible. *Don't say a single, unnecessary word.* This will produce a minor shock; you will feel a compulsive urge to say more. Don't! Do you see what this does? It reveals how much of human conversation is wasteful compulsion. Now you have a fresh self-awareness, which saves energy for inner advancement."

EVERYTHING IS IN YOUR FAVOR FOR WINNING YOUR GOALS

In order to gain esoteric principles and their rewards, we must pay for them in one way or another. This is an interesting cosmic law. Follow carefully and you will see how practical it is, even when seen from the human viewpoint.

Now, the Truth is more valuable than anything else on earth. This means that everything else is of less value. So, in order to get the Truth you must give up something which you now assume is more valuable. This giving up is your payment.

How does it work in practice? True happiness can be gained by paying for it with our vanity, for vanity bars happiness. To be free of torturous envy, we must pay by letting go of those unnatural thoughts which cause envy. For peaceful self-understanding, our payment is to sacrifice our insistence that we already know ourselves.

A woman once came to me with a long tale of woe. What a wonderful time she had in complaining of her mistreatment by others. Do you know people like that? Well, they must pay by giving up their love for their own suffering.

The more and faster you pay, the more and faster you receive permanent riches. So it is to your benefit to see the meaning of this and pay swiftly!

Here is something encouraging. Payment always consists of something harmful to you. So, you see, the whole thing is in your favor. It is like emptying a treasure chest of stones, so it might be filled with jewels.

How a Guilt Complex Was Healed

Ronald H. asked these questions:

Q. I have one of the maladies described in your books, that of a burdensome sense of responsibility, attended by guilty feelings that I am not doing my part in life. Can you cure me?

A. The facts can. Your sense of responsibility is false, created by the illusion that you understand life. The moment you honestly and clearly see that you don't know what to do, release appears. Illusions create false duties, which create false guilts.

Q. But if I see that I don't know what it is all about, I will be scared.

A. Subconsciously, you already know that you do not know, but refuse to face it. Face it, let your fear swell up to consciousness, and it will disappear.

Q. Then will I truly know what life is all about?

A. Certainly. The true is simply an absence of the untrue.

HOW TO BE FREE FROM YOUR ERROR OF SELF

The absorption of cosmic laws enables us to see, for the first time, the kind of world it really is. And it is vastly different from what we assumed.

To live rightly in this world we must first become aware of it. The problem is a man's false assumption that he is already aware, which leaves him with no motive for investigation. Do not assume that the only existing world is that presented by the five senses and the surface mind. Merely to *react* to a strained relationship or to a financial problem is not the same as *understanding* them. Understanding comes from total awareness, which includes the mind and the senses, but is above them.

What Self-Awareness Means

"I wish," said Barbara H., who had come to talk things over, "I knew what is meant by awareness. Could you give me a practical example?"

"Awareness simply means to see things as they really are, and not as our opinions distort them. Take a small blunder and try to see its cause in your impulsiveness, which is a form of unawareness. Maybe you make a stupid remark, which instantly embarrasses you. If you do not defend that remark, but suffer its humiliating effect, you become clearly aware that it *was* stupid. Now, in your clear awareness that it was stupid, and not clever, will you repeat it at some future date?"

"That is what I want," said Barbara with a nod, "something that changes my daily behavior. The last time we talked you gave me another revealing fact. You told me to be aware of the many things I do, not because I want to do them, but because I don't want others to be angry with me. That struck me like lightning, for that is exactly what I was doing. How refreshing to see these things."

Principles governing your mind deserve special attention, for thoughts have power to either reveal or conceal richness. Reflect upon the following points.

Can you be burdened by anything you don't think about, either consciously or unconsciously? How can it be on your back if it is not on your mind? So your aim is freedom from faulty thinking. You may object, "But how can I deal with a difficulty unless I think about it?" The answer is, what we commonly call thinking is not intelligence at all, but only an impulsive stampede of trite reactions and nervous self-assertions. When we think with the true intelligence of self-clarity, the problem ceases to exist, for its very cause was in our mechanical thinking.

If I don't have a compulsive need to appear successful, what do I care if you make more money than I? If I have no unhealthy attraction to shallow social functions, does it bother me if I get no invitations? If I have freedom from fearful dependency upon persons and objects, will I be pained if you no longer wish to be my friend? If my artificial needs fall away through self-insight, do I need to think about these things at all? No. If my false sense of "I" has dissolved, who is there to suffer or complain?

TRANSCENDENTAL LIVING IS A CHEERY ADVENTURE

There is a way out! *Nothing unpleasant need remain as it is.* Difficulties are merely temporary confusions. Face the right direction and you cannot fail to see the rising sun.

You have every reason for good cheer. True cheer is what you feel when your honesty has melted the mental fog, to reveal the open sea. Those who have sailed the open sea for themselves have logged their cheery voyages:

Heraclitus: *"Your destiny changes and brightens as you become more and more a real person."*

C. G. Jung: *"With right self-knowledge, you can cease to be at war with yourself."*

Plotinus: *"A new beauty awaits those with courage to find it."*

Shankara: *"Banish false ideas about yourself, and permanent tranquility follows of itself."*

Dante: *"The deeper contentments which every man seeks can surely be found."*

Huang-Po: *"Nothing, except your own lack of insight, compels you to remain as you are."*

Nicholas Berdyaev: *"Your true duty in life is to set yourself free."*

Sri Aurobindo: *"Through persistent self-work, you will sooner or later feel the definite emerging of your new nature."*

Cosmic Principles of Personal Security

What about cosmic principles regarding personal security?

False security must go if we are to have inner freedom. This is a challenging fact to grasp. It does not mean we must be without material possessions; it means we must not depend upon them for support. It also means we must not cling to acquired beliefs in an effort to feel secure, for clinging breeds fear of loss.

A party of travelers were roaming the countryside. With the exception of one man, they were hopeful of finding a permanent place for secure settlement. But wherever they went, something was displeasing, so they were forced to take to the road once more. One of their worst pains was the confusing decisions necessary when coming to forks in the road. With the exception of the one man, they argued heatedly over the right fork to take, which was usually settled by majority vote.

The exceptional traveler was finally asked why he did not take part in the argumentative decisions. He replied, "To me, it makes no difference. I have no need for a fixed home, therefore, I am home wherever I am."

Do you see the wisdom here?

YOUR REVIEW OF DYNAMIC PRINCIPLES IN THIS CHAPTER

1. Esoteric principles are powers for true conquest.
2. Any earnest person can understand these ideas.
3. Calmness is one reward of esoteric wisdom.
4. Place universal laws before man-made codes.

5. When welcomed, these powers become part of you.
6. Let negative events fall on your clear understanding.
7. Cosmic forces abolish self-slavery.
8. Learn to recognize and value cosmic riches.
9. As we give ourselves up, we win new life.
10. The road ahead leads to true cheerfulness.

5

How to Live Serenely in a Violent World

One thing is certain. The more sane the mind, the more clearly it sees human nature as it is, not as it appears to be on the surface. To expose man's concealed violence has been a major task of men of insight, including the great religious teachers, the philosophers, mystics, poets, writers.

To select a single example, we can review *An Enemy of the People,* by the Norwegian dramatist, Henrik Ibsen.

Dr. Thomas Stockmann, a prominent and highly respected citizen of his town, has made a startling discovery. The local water supply is polluted. Upon informing the town officials of the fact, he is shocked by their attempts to keep him quiet. The officials, including his own brother, the mayor, point out the financial damages they would suffer by revealing the pollution. For one thing, they would lose tourist trade.

The shocked doctor arranges a public meeting, confident that his fellow citizens will back up his attempts at honesty. But his efforts are frustrated from the very start. Finally, when the doctor makes it to the platform, his topic stuns the audience.

He announces his discovery of an evil far greater than polluted water: Human wickedness. Entrenched authorities, he states, possess colossal stupidity and selfishness. Their chief weapons are lies and hypocrisy. It is a social lie that the majority is right, for only a self-liberated individual is right, and he is one in a million.

The doctor's verbal medicine is too distasteful for the audience. Recognizing the truth of his words, they pour upon him all their repressed hatred. Angrily taking a vote, they brand Dr. Stockmann as an enemy of the people.

The final act takes place in the doctor's home. He now has a collection of stones which have shattered his windows. He explains to his wife, "You saw for yourself last night that half the population are out of their minds; and if the other half have not lost their senses, it is because they are mere brutes, with no sense to lose."

Inasmuch as his practice has now been ruined by the so-called pillars of society, Dr. Stockmann and his family plan a new life. It will be a challenge, yes, but what a treasure to be free of social hypocrisy. Besides, the doctor announces his new discovery: "It is this, let me tell you—that the strongest man in the world is he who stands most alone."

HOW TO LIVE FROM YOUR INNER ESSENCE

No doubt you have heard the complaint, "There's no justice in the world. The greedy and the grabby get the desserts, while the good people get crusts."

There are so many errors in this kind of thinking that it would take a book to cover them. Firstly, the world has only sour desserts for the greedy and grabby to get, which an anecdote from Sufism illustrates: An Arab lost his way in the desert. In time, all his food was consumed. He despaired for his life. His heart leaped when he sighted a bag on the ground, for he thought it contained grain. In despair, he found that the bag contained pearls.

Secondly, who are the "good people" who get left out? They are often those who merely have not had the opportunity to behave as wickedly in public as they do in private.

Besides, don't you see that bad people are their own punishment? Don't you see that no one can get away with it? The next time you watch the news on television, closely scan the faces of those whom the world considers to be great and wise. Especially notice those moments when they forget that they are on camera. Watch closely and you may be startled at what you see.

Absorb the answers to these questions from Marie T.:

Q. Have there ever been men with worldly power who also knew the truth?

A. A few, like King Asoka of India and Emperor Marcus Aurelius. One of the early ones was Pharaoh Ikhnaton, who taught that men should live the truth, not talk it. He was opposed, as is always the case, by those having selfish interests in idol worship.

Q. You are right about our immersion in social silliness. I sense this, but why do I still rush into one project after another, most of them stupid and tiring?

A. You fear getting caught without a distraction from your emptiness. You hope that by playing with your toys on the living room floor you won't notice the storm outside. Dare to drop your toys, bit by bit. There will be a temporary increase in anxiety, but with endurance it goes away.

Q. I believe I may run into a difficult situation with other people in a few days. I try to imagine the best way to behave, but need your aid in planning the most advantageous actions.

A. Never set yourself in imaginary situations and try to plan your behavior. This is a vain attempt to feel secure with a fixed plan—which you would not follow anyway. This only calls up a gang of nervous and useless thoughts. Instead, learn to live from your essence. Essence has no need for false aid from memorized plans; it knows exactly what to do in every situation.

HOW TO SEPARATE TRUTHFUL WAYS FROM FALSE WAYS

All false organizations maintain human-level power through the deceitful opposites of *promise of reward* and *threat of punishment*. They can always be recognized by this iron fist in the velvet glove. They start with the promise of and actual delivery of *reward*. It can be anything appealing to human vanity and ignorance—public honors, a vague heaven of some sort, a uniform, a title, and so on. If you fail to fall for the rewards, *punishment* comes swift and sure. They hesitate to do this, for punishment could dangerously expose their pretense of benevolence. But then, they can usually count on human gullibility to take even their cruelty as a sign of strength.

The sick use labels to conceal their sickness. Call it "religion" and the conscience can be lulled long enough to exploit the scared and the weary. Refer to war as "cruel barbarism" and create the cunning illusion that war has an existence outside the vicious stupidity of those who sadly shake their heads over war.

When we break cosmic laws we break ourselves upon them. Cease to break the law which forbids you to lean on human schemes. The people you hope can solve your problems are the very causes of problems.

Don't let them fool you. You are being taken. Don't let them fool you with fancy phrases which are void of true intelligence. Don't let them distract you with sentimental dramatics, for you are always left alone in the dark theater. Don't be deceived by lofty promises of some future paradise, for that only postpones the self-adventure you must take today.

Our self-deliverance will be to the same degree as our self-responsibility.

How Perfect Principles Supply Authentic Answers

Do not overlook the main street which leads to the right ways— the street of self-knowledge. Begin with the plain fact that you do not presently understand yourself, and go on from there. You see, you need not and must not try to deliver yourself from the wicked world. You need only deliver yourself from yourself.

Wayne L. dropped in to say, "At last I see it. The greatest cruelty a man can inflict upon himself is to remain spiritually asleep. I am waking up."

He told me about several small but important successes he had achieved. He said that he finally saw how esoteric principles supply authentic answers to everyday problems. He realized how exterior changes take place as we begin to see ourselves differently. He understood the need for following cosmic realities, not human traditions.

When he asked for a single idea to work with, I told him, "Don't accept comfort at the cost of understanding."

THE BEGINNING OF TRUE WISDOM

A man journeyed a thousand miles to seek acceptance as a student of a Zen teacher. The teacher met him at the door to ask, "What is the first thing you want from your studies?"

The seeker replied, "To be known as a spiritual person."

"Go away," the teacher told him.

"To be able to help others."

"Go away."

"To be happy."

"Go away."

"To have a clear mind."

"Come in."

Until we clear our minds we are no good to ourselves or others, though our vanity fools us into thinking we are such precious little beams of sunshine. When a confused mind tries to do good, it does so with a secret motive of ego-gratification. Reaching out in its own darkness, it mistakes the bottle of poison for medicine, making everyone sick.

Take politics. Do not be dismayed if you cannot understand the arguments of opposing parties on political or social issues. You cannot understand because *there is nothing real in them to understand.* They make no more sense than the babble of small children, playing a game of cowboys and Indians. Both sides argue from ego-serving self-interest. Neither side is really interested in peace or human betterment; their aim is to win their infantile points. By this they hope to blot out their awful fears of being nobodies.

You see, desperate people plead to the world, "Please tell me I am somebody." If only they could see that there is no reply, for none is needed.

Man will prey upon man just as long as he lives unnaturally.

One man gets into a scrape and demands that the next man bail him out. Socially, the reformer preys upon the very miserable people he pretends to love. Sexually, the frustrated man preys upon gullible women. Domestically, spouse unconsciously preys upon spouse, each hoping that the other will somehow serve as a shield from a hostile world.

It is a beginning of true wisdom toward human affairs to perceive the emptiness of society's babble. Only the Third Way of Thinking—which is above human egotism—can create social harmony. As a practical exercise, review the Third Way of Thinking in Chapter 3, connecting it with daily events. It will open your eyes.

HOW TO STOP PLAYING THE PAINFUL GAME OF LIVING

Of course the game is painful. You know that much. But you may not know how to stop. It is as if you are playing a rousing game of tennis with someone who is important in your life, when you grow tired and wish to stop. But your opponent continues to hit the ball, forcing you to continue. Because you don't want him to be disappointed with you, you wearily go on with the game.

To stop, you must risk his displeasure; you must make it clear that you no longer wish to play.

You must see something very clearly. You must see that mankind's game is utterly false. He has false answers, false heroics, false kindness, false intelligence. The whole show is pure nothing. In his vanity a man thinks he is part of the solution, when in fact he contributes to the problem. He lives in a raging madhouse of compulsive desires, which, even if attained, leave him with a tormenting thirst for more. He has no idea of who he is unless another deluded human being tells him, and even then he senses the emptiness of a labeled self.

Perhaps one man in ten million really sees how bad it is. A few have seen it. Jesus denounced hypocrisy. Plato said that awareness of ignorance is the beginning of wisdom. Count Leo Tolstoy called upon men to reject the insane education of sick society.

Krishnamurti has warned against phony ideals which prevent perception of the actual illness. George Gurdjieff taught that deliverance comes only through self-discovery, as did his disciples, P. D. Ouspensky and Maurice Nicoll.

The painful game will stop when we earnestly try to see ourselves as we actually are, and not as we idealistically like to picture ourselves. So we must suspect that we are not who we think we are; we must stop living in dreamland. We can find no better starting point for changing our lives than with a refusal to accept deception, first from ourselves, then from others.

Practical Awareness for Daily Use

You say you want something *practical* for daily use? This is it. If you do not see yourself as you actually are, you will not see others as they really are, so you will be a puzzled victim of both yourself and others. Whoever loves sentimental drama more than reality cannot complain when another actor bumps him off the stage. But when you are real, so is your world, which makes it pleasant.

Now, one of the hardest things for a man to grasp is that it is *superbly good to see the bad.* The badness in itself is not good, but awareness of it is wonderful, for freedom from the painful game results. It is like a doctor's discovery of an illness, which produces healthy treatment.

HOW ONE PERSON AWAKENED FROM A DESPAIR OF LIFE

Harry S. was one of those whose despair expressed itself in suppressed antagonism. This was quite apparent the moment he walked in. All the usual signs of hidden hostility were there, such as a hard expression, which broke itself now and then with suspicious glances around the room.

Knowing that denial of his actual state would be a main point of resistance, I asked whether he understood how badly things were going with him. The question was strong enough to challenge his fixedness, yet not enough to scare him back into his shell. He replied by telling me about his desperate search for answers, covering many years.

We discussed general principles of esotericism for awhile. When he saw I was not about to bite him, his manner relaxed to the point where he could ask questions. I summarize them as follows:

Q. What is the difference between psychology and esotericism?

A. Psychology is fixed on the mental level, that is, it deals only with memorized facts. Esotericism includes *all* of man's parts, such as his wish for trueness and his ability to receive cosmic facts. Psychology can tell you that headaches are often caused by unconscious hostility, but esotericism can show you how to get rid of both.

Q. You say it is folly to submit to human authority, yet you sometimes mention the spirituality of men like Christ and Buddha.

A. There is a vast difference between worshipping the human personality of such men and receiving the truths coming through them. Millions of people worship human personality as a cover for rejecting cosmic impressions. Christ could not qualify for membership in many Christian churches.

Q. Maybe this sounds like a complaint, but I often feel exploited by other people.

A. You *are* exploited. For instance, others know how flattery gives you a pleasurable sensation, which they hope to exchange for what they want from you. When you are no longer a slave to sensation, they can do nothing to you.

Q. You say we need not be upset by mad human power, but doesn't it touch all of us?

A. There is a difference in its having an effect on us and in its causing an upset. Human power is like a low, erratic wind that knocks down some boxes and sets up other boxes for awhile. But it cannot harm the man in the tree top.

Q. Some of the things you say disturb me.

A. Of course they do. That is a principal purpose. How can you awaken from deep sleep unless someone gives you a good shake? Don't resist the shaking, rather, welcome it. How else will you awaken from the nightmare?

HOW TO LIVE YOUR OWN LIFE SERENELY

Harry is a good example of a state which you may find in yourself to some degree. I mean, your ounce of receptivity may be opposed by a ton of resistance. No one by his old nature *wants* to go ahead. We need only to see the necessity for self-work, and go against our own reluctance. The bridge existing between you and your already developed higher centers *can* be crossed with alert work.

Start by being aware that you are not living the way you really want to live. For one thing, notice that you cannot simply get up and walk away from the human mess—as a free man can do—*and as you really want to do*. Wouldn't it be wonderful to live your own life?

A sincere intention is like a magnet. No matter how weak or inconsistent at the start, it begins to attract extra wisdom, brighter views, steady direction, healthy impressions, and more sincere intentions. You really can't lose.

What about outside aid? If you mean business, it will come. It is like a rock collector whose interest urges him up a mountain trail. His own upward walk naturally exposes new and valued rocks to his view. Take the New Testament, which millions read mechanically, without understanding. When read with esoteric insight, it succeeds as a source of cosmic wisdom and good cheer.

It helps to remember that the values of the esoteric world are opposite the values of the human world. Here are three esoteric facts to illustrate the point:

1. *You find your life by losing it:* Human beings try to find what they call "life" with wealth, physical attractiveness, mental movies in which they appear as heroes, and so on. As we lose these false and fleeting values, we make room for trueness.

2. *The present fact is vital, not the future ideal:* If I have a headache, that is what is real about me at this moment. To blissfully dream about banishing my headache a week or year from now is foolish evasion of my present condition. I must admit my present headache if I am to handle it intelligently.

3. *True action arises from mental stillness:* Human actions based in illusion change nothing whatsoever. Place neurotic actors

on a stage having new scenery and they are still neurotic. Only mental stillness can dissolve the illusion that it is a new or beautiful play, after which true action can take place.

TEN ENCOURAGING PRINCIPLES FOR PERFECT LIVING

1. There is a secret place in you that does not feel heartache.
2. You are under no compulsion to accept discouragement.
3. When our intentions are right, a breakdown can lead to a breakthrough.
4. You need never give the slightest thought as to whether or not you appear successful to others.
5. No noise can prevail over the supremacy of inner stillness.
6. Whoever begins to disbelieve in his invented self-image is off on the royal road to trueness.
7. Through esotericism, life finally makes sense.
8. Once you clearly see what is right, you are wonderfully free from the hounding pains of what is wrong.
9. Anything you give up in order to find the inner kingdom will be as nothing to you, once you enter.
10. Everything connected with authentic esotericism is rewarding.

A small child separated from his parents in a crowd will honestly sob out his terror. But mankind is not so honest; it bluffs by pretending that its parents are the ones who are lost. Its frantic bluffs lead to war, crime, alcoholism and every kind of disaster. Clearly, these tragedies are not the basic problems; they are the inevitable results of self-deception. The basic problem is man's alienation from his original nature, which *can* be corrected. There is no alternative to this solution. It is man's frantic insistence upon substitutes which releases the flood of folly upon earth. A few case histories illustrate some secrets of success.

Some Case Histories

Mr. D. wishes to be free from the dreadful drag of the confusions and conflicts of everyday life. He can do so by sticking to the point, which is to suspect his own state of psychic sleep and to shake himself awake.

Mrs. R. simply wants to be a happy woman. She can see that the Eternal Now is forever trying to give her its happiness, but she herself blocks it with thought-barriers of yesterday and to-morrow.

Miss W. cannot understand why her years of religious activities have not done a single real thing for her. She can realize that a single, honest intention to study herself, lasting only a second, is better than fifty years spent in religious ceremonies and charitable activities.

Mr. F. is secretly tormented by desires and cravings. He can extinguish the emotional fires by unmasking frantic desires which cunningly masquerade as authentic needs.

HOW TO FIND FULLNESS IN EMPTINESS

If you go to another person on a non-psychological matter, like buying shoes from a salesman, or getting the aid of a mechanic, there is no problem. You trade your money for his service, and that is the end of it. Your psychic integrity is not compromised.

The Price of Another's Psychic Assistance

But, if you go to another person on a psychological or psychic matter, that person will sense your need of him. Quite unconsciously, he will immediately and subtly try to find ways to make you pay him. It makes no difference what you seek, whether it be love or companionship or acceptance or attention. Your very approach signals him that you need something. He may give it to you, but he will try to figure out how much you are willing to pay. He will make you pay until you are drained, after which he will heartlessly drop you for a fresh prospect.

You must never go to another human being for psychic goods. No one on earth can supply you, though others will make every effort to seem to possess what you need. They do this in order to gain both material benefits and a supply for their own neurotic needs.

Perhaps you say, "But what else can I do? If I do not find comfort and security through others, I will be alone and empty."

Yes, and here is the very salvation you seek. Your discomfort and your insecurity—rightly understood—lead to the ending of discomfort and insecurity. If you see this you will begin to improve.

You did what you did because you thought it would do something for you. You thought it might somehow reduce the awful ache which you don't understand and which never leaves you alone. After awhile, you began to suspect that it was all just another blunder; you are right back where you started. The very suspicion itself was a new pain, for now you must choose between seeing the return of your emptiness or covering it up.

How to Cope with Emptiness Successfully

Let the emptiness return. Let it be there. Do not fear it. Meet it as bravely as you can for now, even if you have but an ounce of heroism. Do not try to conquer the awful ache, but merely be a courageous observer of what is happening to you. Nothing harmful is happening. Even if you think so, nothing harmful can come your way. The very destruction you fear is the destruction of your false self, which means peace at last.

FOREMOST FEATURES OF THIS CHAPTER

1. Observe human nature as it is, not as it appears.
2. To stand alone is to stand with trueness.
3. Self-discovery comes through self-responsibility.
4. Stop playing society's painful game.
5. It is a good thing to see our own badness.
6. You can be inwardly free of the world's follies.
7. It is really possible to live your own life.
8. Esoteric principles supply authentic encouragement.
9. Honest intentions are a great power for you.
10. Start this very moment to release yourself from emptiness of life.

6

How to Swiftly Defeat What Now Defeats You

In order to defeat what now defeats us, we must return to our original intelligence. Without it, every morning automatically sets up a new collision course with grief. Esoterically speaking, what does it mean to be intelligent?

What It Means to Be Intelligent

To be cunning is not to be intelligent. It is stupid to be cunning. The cunning and conniving man has not even the sense to see the self-injury in exploiting others for the sake of his own selfish ambitions.

To be intelligent means to no longer believe in words and labels and slogans. It means to see that loneliness is only a wrong state of mind. It means to admit, "I don't know and never really did." To be intelligent means to cherish self-sincerity, while realizing that sincerity is not as easily attained as imagined. It means to realize that conditioned thinking can only go sideways, never upwards. It means to use each event, no matter how disastrous it seems, as a new key for unlocking a life-mystery. True intelligence is to suspect the existence of an entirely new way to go through life.

To summarize, true intelligence is to work on ourselves correctly. For example, attempts to *reduce* or *evade* a sense of guilt are wrong; efforts to *understand* guilt are right.

A Case History of True Awareness Attained

Clifford B. used his intelligence to detect one area of defeat, exclaiming, "Fantastic! For years I thought I was in command of my own thoughts and actions. But after listening to you I see how easily I am swayed by exterior happenings. Why, the slightest signal turns on a mental riot. What can be done about my suggestibility?"

I pointed out that suggestibility is caused by depending upon confused exterior authorities, who always disagree with each other. Since he does not *know* from his own essence, he must endlessly switch his *beliefs* from one authority to another. We also discussed how suggestibility leads to gullibility, making one a target for sharp-shooting charlatans.

The bright feature was Clifford's awareness of his actual state of suggestibility. He had reached that great state where he no longer wanted to remain with the defeat he had discovered within himself. Clifford was on his way to true mental health, which is true happiness.

Mental health is this: *A man must see that his life is pain and sorrow and fear, and at the same time he must have his first glimpse that it need not remain that way.*

THE MESSENGERS WITH GOOD NEWS

Mankind is like a pair of sleepwalkers who blunder around, creating their own chaos and then suffering from it. One of them may be dimly aware of the stupidity of the other. If it matches his own stupidity, he excuses it, even offers praise. But if it is different from his own, he condemns it in fright. A third person, an awakened man, neither condemns nor approves their actions—he *understands*. He knows they can behave in no other way as long as they walk in their sleep.

So you can see that what is called "justice" cannot exist on the

earthly level. Most human justice comes from judges who condemn their opponent's insanity merely because it is frighteningly
different from their own brand of insanity.

How to Break Away from Psychic Sleep

To say that man dwells in a state of psychic sleep is not simply
a figure of speech. The evidence is plain, if only we will face it.
Would an awakened man burn himself up with angers and hatreds, with egotistical sufferings, with stupid ambitions? *"Towards
the throne they all strive: it is their madness—as if happiness sat
on the throne."* (Nietzsche)

Your task is to break away from all this. Let's see how it can be
done.

Suppose the king of a castle saw a group of approaching riders.
Believing they are about to attack, he attacks them. By not realizing that they are friendly messengers, he refuses admittance,
and so cannot hear their good news. Likewise, messengers from
a higher level seek to deliver good news, but in our misunderstanding we resist and fight.

Most people have such an intense fear of the very truth that
could save them that they crouch behind psychic walls. If they
should encounter a true teacher by accident (perhaps while ac-
companying a friend to a lecture) they immediately fall into
their defenses. One will assume a frozen face, trying not to show
his disturbance. Another, upset over the damage to his ego-self,
will criticize the speaker after the meeting. I have seen this hundreds of times.

You need not defend yourself against anything. Whatever is
true in you does not need defense, and whatever is false must
have no defense. Do not wear yourself out in useless defense,
instead, wisely permit the defeat of falseness. What remains will
be right.

YOUR FIVE MAGIC STEPS TO TRULY VICTORIOUS LIVING

Esoteric wisdom quickly defeats whatever now defeats you.
To gain this wisdom, let's examine the five steps to victory:

1. *The Event*
2. *The Disturbance*
3. *The Endurance*
4. *The Awakening*
5. *The Victory*

Presently, you may understand only the first two steps, that is, an Event of some kind causes Disturbance. This is the limited life of most people, which you will transcend.

Your victorious effort begins with Endurance of the Disturbance. What does this mean? It means to observe the Disturbance, to stand aside and watch as it causes a nervous mind and body. It means you do not try to escape the Disturbance with a defense or an attack; it means you don't explain or complain or resist. You simply *watch.* Endurance means exactly that—to *endure,* to let yourself get shaken up without objection. It helps to remember that what is shaking you is trying to shake you *loose.* It is like shaking sour fruit off a tree to make room for sweet fruit.

As you permit Endurance to have its way, something magical appears. You begin to sense something fresh. You begin to understand that you are not permanently connected with the Disturbance which is your awakening. Then, Victory comes of itself. It happens. It is a real experience.

For instance, suppose an Event causes the Disturbance of feeling lost and empty. By practicing Endurance, you sense an Awakening to the true nature of these feelings, which provides final Victory. When this happens, even once, you will never be the same again. You have the beginning of the true view. And with it comes the ending of agitation, like unhooking yourself from a tractor that has dragged you over bumpy ground.

The Case of a Threatened Financial Position

In the case of Gary W., the Event was an unexpected bill which threatened his financial position. The Disturbance was his nagging worry over it. His Endurance consisted of an effort to see that it was happening only because of his false belief that exterior conditions had power over him, also, to see how pointless it was to feel mistreated by life. His Awakening came by realizing that his essence was free of all outer conditions. His total insight into himself provided refreshing Victory.

SOLVING THE MYSTERY OF DESIRE

We have seen the need for separating true solutions from false ones. Defeat comes by clinging to "solutions" that solve nothing. It is like trying to extinguish fire with oil. Let's see how a true teacher handles those who seek him out.

A true teacher never gives seekers material rewards, nor shallow psychological gratifications, like flattery and excitement. He knows how the cunning nature in man will grasp these as substitutes for truth, which alone can save. His action soon separates the sincere from the insincere. When an insincere seeker's curiosity has been satisfied, he departs. The earnest seeker, sensing something real, remains.

If you should meet a teacher of the blunt type, someone like Socrates or Schopenhauer, you might hear something like this: "For heaven's sake, get rid of your stupid rituals and your pious blabbings, and for the very first time in your life take a good, long, hard, look at yourself and see what a mess you really are. Do this much and I can help you."

How to Attain Success Through Understanding Human Desire

James H. had reached this point. He had finally come to the place where he preferred self-advancement to self-deception. "I would like," he said, "to explore a particular subject which I feel is essential to understand. I refer to *desire*."

James was showing wisdom, for we certainly advance a step closer to supreme success by understanding human desire. The following ideas helped him to break through. Add them to your own supply of helpful facts.

To be whipped through life by subconscious desires and cravings is doing it the hard way. Slavery is certain for the man or woman whose major motive in life is to gratify cravings.

When a desired plan of yours goes wrong, what does it mean?

It merely means that your desire has clashed with reality. It merely means that what you wanted to happen did not happen that way. It does not mean anything else. It does not mean frustration and defeat unless you stubbornly cling to the desire, unless you insist that its fulfillment is necessary to your happiness. It is not necessary, but not seeing this, pain arises.

So we must ask a vital question: Why do we cling so frantically to a desire? Why don't we permit it to be replaced by reality, by what actually happens? Why don't we calmly flow along with events, instead of insisting that they conform to our preferences?

The answer is both shocking and beautiful: *By allowing the shock, we reveal the beautiful.*

YOUR INVITATION TO FREEDOM

The answer above connects with the false sense of self. We wrongly assume that these desires are part of us. Fearing that blockage of these desires means the extinction of the false self, we scream and fight, weep and moan in opposition. All in vain. Reality is what it is, and can never be anything else. It will not and cannot conform to human fancies.

But it offers an invitation to freedom: *The nothingness you fear is the very deliverance you seek.*

So the wise man reverses his position. He no longer tries to destroy what happens with his self-made notions of what should have happened. Instead, he permits truth to destroy his self-centered illusions. Such a man is free.

The next time you are torn between two desires, ask yourself, "Who is this person who is trying to decide?" To your astonishment you will see not one person, but two. One person in you desires this choice and another person desires the other choice. But neither of these is really you; they are merely contrary desires which are *not* you.

The purpose of this experiment is to show you who you are *not.* You are not your choices, nor are you your desires. Now, by abolishing false notions of who you are, the truth appears of itself.

Answers to Questions for Your Better Understanding

The following questions from James H., along with my answers, can add to your understanding.

Q. Why is there so much frustration in desire?

A. Because desire creates its own opposition. The moment you want something of a psychological nature, like approval or attention, you set up a denying force. Can you see this? When there are no such cravings, there is also no opposition, no conflict, which leaves you in peace. Stop and think about this for awhile.

Q. But I want what I want!

A. If you are denied what you want long enough it is likely you will no longer want it. This proves that the so-called value existed in a corner of your mind, not in the object itself. Our task is to explore and sweep out the corners of the mind.

Q. Your book, *The Power of Your Supermind,* is delightfully refreshing, but I don't understand certain ideas. You say we should have no concern for results. But I crave bright outcomes!

A. You call a certain result bright because you hope it will confirm false values you have about yourself. This causes fear, for if results are contrary, your imaginary self has no support. By dropping fanciful ideas about yourself, you are indifferent to results, for they can neither add nor take away. Can gold or lack of gold affect a soaring eagle?

TEN PROFITABLE QUESTIONS TO ASK YOURSELF

How quickly can we defeat what now defeats us? With the same speed that we succeed with our minds. Let's take an example of non-successful thinking. A man foolishly thinks he can somehow dilute his fear by sharing it with others. So we have the pathetic spectacle of everyone pouring his cup of fear onto his neighbor's head, while getting doused in return by his neighbor.

Here is an instance of successful thinking. You love someone only when you truly understand him. This means we must first understand ourselves, which requires self-unity, with no self-contradictions. Your own oneness naturally encloses the other, effortlessly and without personal motive of self-gain. Love has no fixed point; it flows unceasingly, covering everything along the way, just as a stream encloses the boulders in its path. This is not a sentimental idea; it is a fact.

If the lights in your house go out, what do you do? You check your own home to see what is wrong; you don't blame your neighbor. Likewise, when you feel defeated, examine your mental household for defects. The defects exist in the mind, and nowhere else. There might be an outside crisis, but your reaction is always *your* reaction. There is a way to be different from how you now are.

When people come to me with their questions, I often find it good to reply with certain questions for their own study. Here are ten such questions for your own consideration.

1. Can you see shocks and sufferings as alarm clocks which try to awaken you?

2. How are you going to silence the inner chaos with your old ways, when you have not succeeded throughout the years?

3. Do you understand the esoteric fact of giving up everything in order to win everything?

4. Who is going to save you if you don't?

5. Have you considered the possibility that you may be thinking your problems into existence?

6. Why have you not thrown all your cares upon the Truth itself, where they truly belong?

7. Did it ever occur to you that you can quietly stand aside and observe a panicky thought, instead of being carried away by it?

8. Do you understand how hidden antagonism blocks psychic growth, which means it also blocks happiness?

9. Do you know that the only important question is whether you are earnestly working to change yourself?

10. Why don't you make up your mind to break away from all that has kept you a prisoner up to now?

PRACTICAL PLANS FOR DAILY SKILLFUL LIVING

How a Prominent Person Achieved His Greatest Success

Floyd F. had achieved success in his business and in local politics. He was an active man, always on the run. "But I am no longer young," he told me, "and have reached the age where I must give some thought to philosophic matters. I have been nagged for a long time by the feeling that I have been playing games with myself. I think you know what I mean. Why am I so driven to get things from life, which get me nothing?"

"We try to get something only when we feel we lack it. But what you seek is not outside yourself. If you have an apple in your hand, you do not look for one in the apple orchard. That is what the whole world is doing. Everyone falsely assumes that there is a great big, wonderful apple orchard somewhere out there. To cover this fearful illusion they invent artificial apples which they miserably exchange with each other."

"As you know," Floyd continued, "I am prominent in business and government. Can you connect what you say with my affairs? What I mean is, if I am playing games with myself, how can I stop?"

With this inquiry I was able to supply him with a practical esoteric fact, as follows: "The next time you frantically feel you must get something in order to win an advantage, ask yourself exactly *who* will get the advantage? This *who* which you take as yourself does not exist; it is an imaginary self. So how can it get any advantage? How can an imaginary bucket get imaginary water? Do you begin to understand the game you are playing with yourself?"

"Faintly," he replied, then went on, "I have read what you say about being a conscious person. How does this connect with my nervous rushing around?"

"A man may think he rushes at a task because he loves it or because he is so efficient. But usually, he rushes to get it done because of the very opposite, that is, he doubts his abilities. This forces him to try to banish his doubts and his tensions by finishing as soon as possible. The solution is to slow down, make the doubt conscious, and endure it fully. This will dissolve self-doubt, for it has a false foundation, as do all anxieties."

Floyd nodded. "So *that's* the answer. What a wonderful revelation. We do *nothing*, kidding ourselves into thinking it is *something*."

"We can stir the cup of tea all day long but it won't taste sweet without the sugar. Your sugar is your inner essence."

Floyd smiled, said with a sigh, "Well, I see I have a new project for the weeks ahead. I know very well you are right. I will come again, if I may. Thanks."

HOW TO WIN SUPREME PSYCHIC SUCCESS

How long must one experience defeat? As long as one prefers the illusion of individual separation to the reality of Universal Unity. To say the same thing in another way, we must return to ourselves. Plotinus gave the illustration of a man so covered with mud that his natural attractiveness could not be seen. The mud, which is foreign to his true nature, must be washed away if he is to see his original self.

Man thinks about the wrong things, but can become aware of doing so. He lets his mind wander into dark jungles of hostility, but he can find the way out. He wastes his mental money on trifles, but can cease to squander. We need only realize our possession of abundant mental money, which we have been spending foolishly. Awareness of mental foolishness is the beginning of wise mental investments.

There is a certain kind of inner declaration providing power to defeat whatever now defeats you. Ralph Waldo Emerson made this victorious declaration:

> *You think it is because I have an income which exempts me from your day-labor, that I waste (as you call it) my time in sun-gazing and star-gazing. You do not know me. If my debts, as they threaten, should consume what money I have, I should live just as I do now: I should eat worse food, and wear a coarser coat, and should wander in a potato patch instead of in the wood—but it is I, and not my twelve hundred dollars a year, that love God.*

The entire matter of freedom can be resolved by anyone. All a man needs is to ask earnestly and persistently, "Am I living from my adopted notions or from *myself?*" Supreme psychic success is won by realizing who you truly are.

Here are aids in question and answer form:

Q. Why can't we trust in human nature to make everything right at last?

A. You do not know human nature as it really is. Suppose the rumor spread around the world that a comet was about to collide with the earth. The churches would overflow with praying and humble people. But five minutes after the rumor was proved false, you would again see everyone at each other's throats.

Q. How can we change unpleasant facts about ourselves?

A. By seeing and accepting them as unpleasant facts. We must not evade them with self-pictures of being such angelic blessings to mankind that any improvement is unthinkable.

Q. Does success exist on the human level?

A. There is a condition which is labeled as success, but it is powerless to bring happiness. It is neither good nor bad, right nor wrong to succeed in worldly projects. What is self-defeating is to identify with either success or failure, and to try to get a feeling of self from them.

Q. You say we can be free of all painful competition. If only I could grasp this!

A. Competition exists only between human egos, so if ego is extinguished, a sense of competition is impossible. Work for your living, but don't compete with others in the working world for honors or favors. If *you* suffer from a sense of competition, who has the problem, who pays the price, and who can work toward liberation?

HOW TO END ALL SUFFERING

Let's take a defeat that casts down millions of people—suffering. What is the cause of suffering? Can it be ended? We can find the esoteric answers with an illustration.

Picture yourself standing on a grassy knoll overlooking a broad river. In a peaceful state of mind, you watch the passing ships. They appear upstream, pass in front of you, and disappear downstream. In an impersonal manner, you enjoy their coming and going.

Suddenly, a costume-clad stranger appears at your side. He tells you something you find hard to believe. He promises that every ship passing in view will become your personal possession. Your very sighting of a vessel insures your permanent possession of its peoples and cargoes. With that, he vanishes.

Even though it sounds strange, you want to believe him. So you excitedly scan the river for the ships you hope to own.

Presently, a ship appears, laden with rare and costly woods, including cedar and mahogany. A moment later another ship comes into view, loaded with dozens of famous people, including politicians and film stars. Other ships appear with their attractive cargoes.

But now you are aware of something. A change has taken place in your mind and feelings. They are no longer pleasantly relaxed, as was the case when you merely watched the passing drama. You are now anxious toward the ships. You worriedly wonder whether they are really yours; you impatiently wish they would turn in your direction as the stranger promised; you are fearful that someone else might claim them.

You are dropped into deeper despair by the next event. One by one, the ships you hoped to own, pass slowly from sight. You are left sad, confused and with feelings of being cheated. But this is followed by an intelligent realization: The stranger's promise was false. Even so, it was your eager acceptance of the trickery that caused the damage. Because you gave up your original quietness for vague promises of possession, you caused your own sorrow.

You have awakened. You see what happened. Now you know better. You are no longer tense toward the ships, for you see where peace really exists. It exists within your free self and nowhere else. And so you enjoy your own liberty, which no person and no event can ever take away.

With us, the river is life. The ships and cargoes are the events and people who come and go. The stranger is our own set of illusions, including those accepted from other confused people. The despair is caused by clinging to the untrue. The awakening is what defeats whatever may now be defeating you.

SUCCESSFUL IDEAS FROM THIS CHAPTER

1. Our original intelligence can win true success.
2. Extend your welcome to esoteric good news.
3. Use the Five Magic Steps to true esoteric victory.

4. We must understand the nature of desire.
5. We can be free of all false and painful desires.
6. Your life brightens as you succeed with your esoteric mind.
7. Love is a state of total understanding.
8. Whatever the difficulty, it can ultimately be defeated.
9. Supreme psychic success can be won by you through esotericism.
10. Suffering ends as we see life as it is in esoteric truth.

7

How Your Revealed Powers Provide You with New Self-Command

Bruce W. sank back in the large, comfortable chair and told me of his many achievements over the years. He emphasized his rise to leadership in the various organizations he had joined. He was president of the local club for businessmen, and was an officer in both his church and political group. He said he had a flair for speaking out forcefully on almost any subject, which attracted attention. He admitted that he often spoke more from bluff than from understanding, but it was still a good way to appear authoritative.

As Bruce went on, his voice faltered now and then, revealing an inner struggle. He sensed that even now, while talking with me, he was performing his act of confident authority. Now and then he made an effort to break it off, but it grabbed him once more and carried him away. He was like a passenger on a runaway bus, dreading the ride, but unable to get off.

After going over his successes once more, he slowed down somewhat, to finally ask, "Now that I've arrived, where am I?"

I asked, "Is the inner life of enough interest to you for a patient and thorough exploration?"

"I have always been an eager reader," he replied, "which is how I got in touch with you. I have read all your books, which appeal to me because of the simple way they present these deep ideas. Since reading is my strong point, maybe I can use it as an opening to something better. I know there is the right way and the wrong way to read about esoteric facts. Do you have suggestions?"

Acquired Knowledge Not the Whole Answer

"Remember that knowledge is only one of the necessary ingredients for self-transformation. Since it is fairly easy to read books and collect facts, many people are willing to do this much. However, they stop at this point, falling into the trap of identifying with their acquired knowledge."

Bruce responded, "I'm not sure I know what that means."

"It means they take pride in their collected facts; use them for ego-satisfaction, instead of for growth. They proudly place their knowledge in the window, just as a merchant displays his goods. It is easy to spot a person in this trap. He loves to preach, to let you know how much he knows. Inwardly, he has a self-image of being an intellectual, a thinker. He is nothing of the sort; he is a mechanical man, loaded with hidden vanity and arrogance—and woe to anyone who tries to point it out."

Bruce asked, "How can I avoid this trap?"

"To repeat, knowledge is only one of the needed ingredients. You cannot bake a cake with flour alone. You must take this flour—your knowledge—and let it jolt you out of your old ways. This permitted jolting adds another essential ingredient—the willingness to face yourself as you actually are. For instance, you might willingly see how much you really dislike the people you pretend to like. Your willingness eventually destroys the *pride* of having knowledge, which then releases the knowledge to operate on its own useful level."

"You know, Mr. Howard," Bruce concluded, "I never had the slightest suspicion that there was so much to this. I can see why you say we are all asleep. All right, I'll let it shake me awake!"

HOW TO WIN GENUINE SELF-COMMAND

Do we want evidence of the correctness of these principles? Do we want confidence in their power to deliver newness? Everything that happens to us is perfect evidence of their power and accuracy. The evidence is so overwhelming we fail to see it. You are struck by a severe disappointment? It is because your desire clashed with what actually happened, so you must learn to place reality before preference. You cannot see why your happiness does not rise to the heights? It is because there are many things you do not understand as yet, but which await your insight.

The Fallacy of Living for "Getting"

The lives of almost everyone revolve around the axle called *getting*. People think that if they could just get this or that—love, security, prominence—all would be well. And so they struggle in the whirlpool of their own cravings. Esotericism can pull them out, for it has a fresh definition of *getting*. Esoterically, to *understand* is to *get*. In this newness there is no striving nor failure, only ease, contentment, and serenity.

Let's see how a new understanding provides right relationships in the world you inhabit.

The ancient Roman emperors kept their citizens in unconscious slavery by giving them "bread and circuses." The chains today are more refined and difficult to detect, but the "slaves" still feel them.

Watch, watch very carefully how a false society operates. False human power must depend upon blackmail, violence, flattery, conspiracy, ritual, threat, and so on. In other words, human evil needs the assistance of other human evil. Spiritual power has none of these; it is above human neurosis and crafty schemes. True power has no human backing at all, yet is backed up by the entire universe, of which you are a part.

Now, the worst thing that can be done toward human evil is to compromise with it and reward it. To reward evil is to increase it. But evil people reward other evil people because they either fear them or wish a reward in return. This is what cowardice really is. It takes a man of authentic integrity to refuse to reward evil. This is what heroism really is.

You see, if you fear a malicious man, he will sense it and

gleefully take advantage of you. Your fear supports his illusion of personal power. But if you refuse to fear him, he will either hate or ignore you, but *you have been true,* and that is the only thing in the world that matters.

A machine is told what to do. You can order a machine to destroy people, to slave endlessly in dreary deserts, to bear heavy burdens on its back. A machine will obey because it has no mind; it can only react with its mechanical nature. It will labor for anyone, anytime, until worn out and discarded.

But you are not a machine. You are a human being. You have a mind capable of shaking off the control buttons forced onto you by a brutal society. You can think for yourself. You can have self-command. You can do what *you* want to do.

Is that worth understanding?

THE UNIVERSAL LANGUAGE OF PSYCHIC UNDERSTANDING

I recall a certain individual whom I met several years ago whose life could be described with one word: *ruination.* His language at that time was that of bitterness and desperation. But no more. He now speaks a new language, which I will explain to you.

If the only language a man speaks is English, that is also the only language he understands. You cannot speak to him in French or German. If you talk to him in French, telling him of a treasure buried in his own yard, he will never own that treasure, for your words are meaningless to him.

Now, every human being on earth speaks a certain psychological language. It is useless to speak to him in any language but the one he lives by. If his language is that of violence, you must not speak to him in the language of reason, for he can only react in violence against reason. If he speaks the language of self-pity, any attempt to communicate with him in the language of self-reliance will be scorned.

Almost no one understands this fact of human nature, which is why all attempts to solve social problems fail utterly. Those who understand the least are those who claim to understand the most.

Those speaking the language of Esotericism understand each other to the degree of their own command of the language. Those speaking the low-level language of Egotism cannot understand each other, but don't realize that they are not in communication. The language of Egotism has a million strange dialects.

So a man's language-level must be considered when dealing with him. This means we must realize his present confinement to his own level of understanding. To a degree, parents understand this with their children.

The language of Egotism splits itself into opposing camps, both of them equally destructive, which means this: People speaking this language either hate each other or exchange shallow sentimentalities labeled as love. Such people turn viciously on each other at the slightest stab to their vanity.

You can learn the new language of Esotericism. In fact, you are learning it right now, as you read these pages. One benefit will be an understanding of others, even if they don't understand you. You will know when to speak and when to be silent, what person to invite and what person to keep out of your life.

With patient learning, you will grasp what this new language is trying to tell you. It is trying to tell you about a tremendous treasure in your own yard.

THE WAY TO TRUE INDEPENDENCE

Consider this strange human situation.

Most people feel comfortable only when *compelled* to do this or not to do that. Like sheep, they willingly place themselves under man-made rules and customs. Why? Otherwise they would have to do the one thing they fear most of all—*to think for themselves.* They fear their own freedom! It is much more comfortable, they think, to obey some smooth faker who calls himself an authority. If something goes wrong, they can always blame their leader, which they will do, sooner or later.

Do you still think humanity is sane? Do you still think the habitual ways can ever change anything? Or must each individual bravely discover the truth for himself?

Since man refuses his own freedom, he can have no complaint

when the dictators, political or otherwise, wrap him in chains. He has asked for it. But he can stop asking any time he chooses.

Almost all claims of independence are pitiful self-deception. Look at your relatives and friends. You know how unfree they are. But true independence is possible. There is a way to achieve it. True independence comes when we cease to *force* and start to *flow*. The truly independent man knows and lives with cosmic laws, which release him from cramping human codes.

What you need to do is to wake up. To wake up means to snap your mental movies a dozen times a day, fifty times a day, until you see the difference between mental movies and simple awareness of what is going on.

Harvey D. started a question and answer session pertaining to his difficulties:

Q. How do false leaders attain power in the first place?

A. False leaders cannot exist without false followers.

Q. I feel as if people are judging me.

A. When anyone judges you, look to see who is judging. But don't do it angrily; realize that judges are attempting to escape their own self-judgment, which pronounces them guilty.

Q. One part of me wants to abandon this old, stupid self, but another part clings anxiously to it.

A. Yes, that is how it is. You may now wonder how you can live without the old self, but the time may come when you wonder how you ever lived with it.

Q. I feel whipped by my own thoughts. How can I find relief?

A. When a man does not know what to think, he seeks relief by thinking about *anything*, which prevents authentic relief. Relief from torturing thoughts comes when you willingly abandon all effort to force answers.

Q. As directly as possible, please tell me how to find newness.

A. Permit yourself to remain in conscious conflict until it destroys something useless in you.

Q. How can we find more opportunities for inner enrichment?

A. Enrichment comes by conscious attention to the constant crises within you. Everyone has hundreds of crises every day, so the earnest person has hundreds of opportunities.

Q. Give us an encouragement!

A. The Answer exists!

YOU CAN WIN THE SPARKLING NEWNESS OF FULL LIFE

All by itself, the following esoteric secret can lead you to newness.

Every one of your human relationships must be on your terms or not at all. Now, be very careful not to misunderstand this profound fact. If you have desires to get anything of a psychological nature from another, the relationship is not on your terms at all, but on the terms of your acquired desires. So your desires—for relief from loneliness, for someone to talk to—are in charge, not you. There is no true communication in this; only the exchange of mutual desires. And where this dominates, the relationship will have subtle conflict, and certainly no love.

What must you do? Never trade yourself with others. Do not trade your potential psychic freedom for the false comfort of another's company. Not only will loneliness persist, but you will have wandered a greater distance from yourself. Perhaps you feel insecure. Do not seek out those who cover up their own insecurity with the same beliefs which have kept you afraid. That is the same as trading counterfeit money. You don't have to live this way at all.

Shall I tell you what you really want? Yes, you would give up everything you possess to attain it.

What you really want is the NEW.

You sense what the New is. You sense it because you can compare it with the familiar old, which you see all around you. The old is tension, disturbance, unnaturalness, terror, craving, trickery, gossip, fawning, agitation, boasting, depression, fighting, falsehood, dullness, suspicion, ignorance, sorrow.

The sparkling NEW is what you really want. And I will tell you how to win it. The New emerges from your own receptivity to the:

Unseen

Untried
Unknown
Unusual
Unfamiliar
Unnoticed
Unwanted

The *unwanted!* When you finally want what you presently do not want, you become a different person. The New is not what you *get,* but who you *are.*

THE POWER OF PURE FEELING

People sense the need for emotions which work in harmony, not in opposition. Grant Y. was one of those who saw the need for drastic change in a particular emotion—that of a bad temper. "I have tried," he told me, "to connect my anger with the ideas you are teaching us. So far I have seen a few helpful things."

I asked, "What have you observed?"

"Well, I see the mechanicalness of anger. Someone says something I don't like and bang, up it flares, like a struck match. Funny, but before I am aware of its approach, there it is, burning me."

"To see just that much is progress. The time can come when you will see anger creeping up, ready to spring. It is a curious experience, and valuable. Do you see the necessity of faithful self-observation?"

"Yes, because it prevents mechanicalness from taking charge of me. The cougar is still there, ready to spring, but I'm getting onto his ways. The time will come when he will no longer catch me unaware."

We discussed another feature of bad temper, that of its contagious nature. One person in a bad mood can easily infect others in the home or office, without anyone realizing what is going on. One great gain made by the student of esotericism is that he ceases to fall victim to such psychic punishments. No outsider dictates his feelings; *he lives from himself.*

"That alone," Grant remarked as we concluded our talk, "is worth the price of admission to esotericism."

How Feeling Is Genuine Understanding

Let's examine another area of our emotional life.

Do you understand the need to *feel* a truth as well as to *know* it? To know with feeling is to know truly. I am speaking of true feeling, which is pure, having no sensationalism. I want to present you with one of the most mysterious of all esoteric secrets. When solved by you, the mystery turns into a practical power. As you read it, *do not try to comprehend with the mind alone,* for thought by itself is incapable of penetration. Rather, enter into its significance with your *total self:*

> Dismiss those with strength and you have strength.
> Ignore what parades as morality and there is morality.
> Cease talking about love, and love will appear.
> Banish what is labeled as success and we have success.
> Cancel what is called wisdom and there is wisdom.
> Get away from those who know best and you know best.
> Stop preaching about peace and peace occurs.
> Do not desire a miracle and a miracle happens.

Relax. Let go. Absorb. Do you feel the inner meaning?

WHAT YOU MUST DO TO GAIN PERFECT UNDERSTANDING

At this point in the book, do you see the problem? Do you see that everything is purely personal? The problem must be solved where it actually resides—within the man. The difficulty does not exist in a cruel social system; it exists in the individual who unconsciously participates in and promotes the tragic system. The problem does not exist in failure to win a desired goal; it exists in men and women who do not understand what life is all about.

Please do not believe that you already understand this. It is much deeper than you think, and vastly richer than you can imagine.

How does a problem-person get that way? *Isolation!* There is no better word to describe what we are trying to understand. Picture in your mind a man who has isolated himself within a transparent covering. Surrounded by this shield, isolated by it, he works, marries, plans, passes his days—and agonizes.

He assumes that his shield is his protection, when in fact, it is his desolation. Trying to keep back anguish and loneliness, he has enclosed himself with them. He is his own prisoner.

To protect is to perish; to expose is to endure.

We must expose ourselves fully to life's experiences. Nothing is discovered in isolation, any more than a rainbow is discovered in a closet. To harmonize with life we must be with it altogether, without resistance, with no concern for what it may bring us.

Break out. That is what you must do. Break out from behind your shield of self-protection.

Always remember that you are trapped only by your wrong thought toward a situation, never by the situation itself. This does not mean that you necessarily remain in an unwanted position; it means you must first see your own faulty thinking toward it. Unless this is done, you will merely leap from the battered ship into the stormy sea.

An anxious attempt to destroy enemies must certainly fail. Don't try to destroy enemies, whoever or whatever they are. Even if you succeed, you fail, for they disappear only to be replaced by other adversaries, as your experience has shown you. This forces you into battle after battle until you are worn out.

The right way is to let enemies destroy themselves. You start by seeing that enemies are not external to you. No, your enemies are not cruel people or frustrating conditions. It only appears so because you do not as yet understand. But you can start all over with a fresh mind. You can replace *thinking* with *knowing*.

How?

This is a good place to review the three supreme steps for daily success, supplied in Chapter 1:

1. *We must deeply see the need for self-transformation.*
2. *We must see ourselves as we actually are.*
3. *We must work earnestly with esoteric principles.*

HOW TO ACQUIRE THE COMPETENCE OF SIMPLICITY

Mr. and Mrs. Jeffrey G. came to me to say they wanted to get away from it all. They had heard of some attractive islands where life was less demanding, where they could blend with events, instead of fighting them. The islands, they explained, were not too far from civilization, so all the necessary services were handy. Still they wondered whether it was the right move to make. Asked Mr. G., "What about this yearning for simplicity? Are we thinking clearly?"

We discussed that widely sought but seldom found jewel called simplicity. Nature itself teaches the way to simplicity. Look at that tree on the hillside. Do you see ornaments? Is it trying to be taller than the next tree? Does it feel sorry for itself? The tree is complete because it is exactly what nature intends it to be— ITSELF.

No, this is not merely philosophy; it is practical fact. The point is to see our inability to be simple while separated from our original nature. What separates us? Unnatural desires do.

But we have power to think, so let's use it to think profitably toward simplicity. Simplicity is the same thing as happiness. That makes it worth seeking. It is the same as sanity and health and energy. That is what we need.

Simplicity comes to the clarified mind, whether on an island or not. It comes when we no longer need to prove ourselves.

How to Secure the Happiness of Simplicity

Mr. and Mrs. G. asked these questions:

Q. You say that the happiness of simplicity comes by abolishing conditioned desires, but it makes me happy to get what I want.

A. Does it? You are not happy because of attainment, but because your desire is temporarily at rest. What happens to desire upon attainment? It disappears, banishing the nagging pain, but only temporarily. Mechanical desire always returns. Let consciousness replace mechanicalness. If you want to save years of confusion, understand this.

Q. How can I make the truth operate for me?

A. Once the truth is truly seen, let it alone and it operates for you. You and the truth are not separate; you are One. You block yourself by trying to use the truth, which is above human effort. By receptivity, the truth flows within, carrying you along.

Q. How can we tell when we are unaware of ourselves?

A. Nothing is simpler. Whenever you feel worried, nervous, pressured, you are living from imagination, not from awareness. These negativities do not control a conscious man.

Q. I have frightful dreams. What do they mean? How can I get rid of them?

A. Dreams are thoughts you don't know about during the day. They have value in revealing contradictions between what you think you think and what you actually think. As consciousness increases, dreams decrease.

THE PERFECT WAY TO SELF-COMMAND

What if you wasted your automobile battery by leaving the lights on during the day? It is similar waste when we employ our mental powers for useless activities. The mind regains its original power by stopping wastage. Catch yourself during your day. What useless thoughts drain psychic energy? Could it be a mental movie of how badly someone mistreated you? You are being emotional over a problem, instead of trying to understand it.

Allan H. asked me for a way to conserve his energy when thinking of esoteric matters. He admitted how much his mind wandered away from essential points. I provided him with a list of ten key words of esotericism, for his daily review and reflection. You can also save energy by keeping these key words in mind:

1. *Naturalness*
2. *Receptivity*
3. *Self-renewal*
4. *Now*
5. *Insight*
6. *Persistence*
7. *Watchfulness*
8. *Self-unity*
9. *Patience*
10. *Genuineness*

At another session Allan said, "I feel kicked around. I want command of my own life."

"To achieve this," I replied, "you must voluntarily pass through a stage where you have lost everything which you now call command."

"What do you mean?"

"Look at almost anyone you know. He believes he has original ideas, that he thinks for himself, that he is strong and wise. Yet he *lives* in a whirlwind of troubles. Is he in command of himself, as he assumes? Of course not. Yet he fails to see the slightest contradiction between his fantasies about himself and the way he actually is. This is the false kind of command which must disappear."

"But if I let go of what I think is self-command I will have nothing left of my former self."

"Which is your exact aim. I know this is difficult to grasp, but stick with it. You see, esoterically, absence of habitual control is true control."

"You are saying, I think, that cosmic command takes over with the abandonment of conditioned command."

"There you have it."

Allan nodded. "At least I see one thing. I used to think that ownership of people and property gave me command. Thanks to you, I now know better."

"You may write your name on a kite, but the wind will still carry it away. But it makes no difference what the wind does with our kites."

"I understand."

SPECIAL IDEAS OF THIS CHAPTER

1. Self-command comes through independent thinking.
2. The language of esotericism is rich in meaning.
3. You have abundant opportunities to find newness.
4. Newness comes from the unseen and the unusual.
5. You can learn to live from yourself.
6. Try to feel the truth, as well as know it.
7. Your task is to break out of the old nature.
8. Live simply and naturally.
9. Let esotericism supply your new life-command.

8

How You Can Awaken to New Feelings of Supreme Happiness

What the average man calls his happiness is merely a short and shaky truce between past and future miseries. He fearfully wonders how long he can escape exposure, for he knows full well the vast difference between his public smiles and his private dreads. He feels compelled to run hard all day, just to keep from losing what he has. His brand of happiness is no happiness at all.

Above artificial happiness is true contentment, of which he is as yet unaware. Teachers of Eastern wisdom call it *ananda*, meaning *bliss*. You can take a step toward *ananda* with the help of the following illustration.

Picture a man taking an evening stroll, when a heavy fog rolls over town. As he gropes his way back home, a business associate appears out of the fog to ask him a complicated question about finances. The man replies, "I can't think clearly about it until I get out of this fog." Later, he meets a salesman who tries to sell him something. The man speaks out, "I cannot consider your products until I get home." A block later he meets his doctor who warns him against driving himself so hard. The man replies, "I must get out of this fog before I can understand your advice."

That man is wise. He sees the need for doing things in their right order.

Do *you* see the impossibility of right thought and action while immersed in psychic fog? Can you admit that you actually do not know what you are doing? That is *intelligence*. That is the first and foremost business in life. And it is the motivating force for leading you out of the earthly fog and into your psychic home. Then, in that clearness, you will know exactly what to do about everything.

HOW MYSTIC WISDOM PROVIDES TRUE GUIDANCE

After Marjorie S. and I had discussed her difficulties, she explained, "My chief unhappiness is that I just don't know what to do with myself."

I asked, "Why do you need to know?"

She puzzledly replied, "I don't understand what you mean."

"You say you do not know what to do with yourself. This means you temporarily have no distraction from your own emptiness. Even when you find one, that distraction will last only as long as the activity, after which you will again not know what to do with yourself. Do you like this vicious circle?"

"No, but what can I do?"

"You can understand your error in assuming that doing or achieving will cancel the anxiety of not knowing what to do."

"But what will cancel it?"

"Self-understanding, which includes insight into your need to be on the move every minute."

"Then will I know what to do?"

"In your *psychological* life there will be no need to know, for life rolls forward of itself, with no concern on your part. This is a new kind of esoteric wisdom, which guides you accurately in exterior matters also."

Marjorie nodded. "There is something great about all this, but I need time to absorb it. Please give me a minute to make a couple of notes. I want to think it over at home."

After making a few notes she asked me to state the same facts in a new way, so I told her, "There is nothing to fear in not knowing what to do with yourself; fear arises only when you anxiously try to escape the void with a contrived activity. The void is really your happiness—you run from your very happiness in a wrong effort to find happiness."

We must understand that happiness cannot be found by *choosing* this or that course from our bank of fixed memories. Choosing implies that this or that course must certainly be the right one, and that in time we will hit the bell of happiness. But what if *all* our choices are wrong? What if we begin to suspect that *all* our acquired bells can only strike false tones? With that intelligent suspicion we are *forced* to abandon them, and should gratefully do so. When false tones no longer block your hearing, the true becomes audible. With this inward simplicity, the exterior world loses its power to baffle you, for, *"This simplicity expands itself little by little to outer things."* (François Fénelon)

THE PSYCHIC "SILENT SEEING" VICTORY

A shepherd once lived and tended his flock on a broad and sunny meadow. However, at the edge of the meadow were deep and dark valleys in which roamed a special breed of fierce wolves. From time to time the wolves climbed out of their dark valleys to attack the shepherd's flocks. He did everything possible to protect his sheep, but was no match for the cunning wolves.

When the attacks had first begun, the shepherd had tried to fight them off with whatever weapons he had, but in vain. Next, he had offered up a prayer for protection, but the wolves still came. Another time he had sought aid from neighboring shepherds, but saw that they were just as much at the mercy of the wolves as he was. Finally, in total despair, he tried to pretend that the wolves did not really exist, but was horrified at the even greater conflict caused by his self-deception. It made him irritable, nervous, gloomy.

After enduring the misery for a long time, an idea flashed into his mind. Perhaps he needed an entirely fresh approach to the problem. *Perhaps insight into the nature of the wolves would provide new wisdom for handling them.* He decided to pursue this fresh idea.

So the next time the wolves came up from their dark valleys, he studied them through the window. Then, with growing boldness, he stepped outside for a closer look. To his great astonishment, the more he bravely faced the wolves, the less fierce they became. His understanding of their nature had a magical effect upon their behavior. They became weaker and less violent. Also, as he steadfastly watched the wolves over the passing weeks, they appeared less frequently. Finally, they disappeared altogether, leaving the shepherd and his flocks in peace and safety.

The shepherd is every man or woman on earth. The wolves are those fierce thoughts roaming the subconscious valleys of the mind. The defeats are the false ways of handling the wolves. The right way is a courageous consciousness that probes the very nature of the wolves. This victory is possible for every man or woman.

How is victory attained?

By practicing *Silent Seeing.*

HOW "SILENT SEEING" HELPS YOU

Silent Seeing is a combination and simplification of all the techniques for freedom set down by the ancients, including Buddha and Socrates, and modern teachers, Carl Jung and William James among them.

It is the simplest technique imaginable, yet needs faithful practice, for that is what delivers astonishing results. Silent Seeing consists of observing your thoughts and feelings as they enter, pass by, and exit. You do nothing whatsoever with them; you merely observe. You observe your thoughts *silently,* that is, without judgment, without pain or pleasure, without acceptance or rejection. You impersonalize, you do not call them your own thoughts, any more than you would claim ownership of a flock of birds passing across the sky.

Let's connect this in a practical way with one kind of self-torment endured by millions of unaware people. It is the raging thought, "I have been cheated by life; other people don't give me what I rightfully deserve; I give so much and get so little."

What nonsense! What a cruel hoax to play on oneself! The only thing that cheats a man is his own delusion of being cheated. Even if his bad manners win his demands he soon becomes a victim of a new neurotic need. So these thoughts burn him in a hell of his own making.

Silent Seeing can free him. First, he can see that these thoughts actually dominate his mind. Next, he can calmly detach himself from them by letting them arise and pass away of themselves. Finally, he can *refuse to enjoy them;* yes, for he has found a twisted satisfaction in his torment, for it supplies a False Feeling of Life. Practiced faithfully, the fires of his own mental hell will fade out, just as fire in a fireplace goes out for lack of fuel.

Whatever happens to you is not the important thing. The vital feature is to watch passively whatever happens. Remain calmly unaffected by the occurrence, just as a movie screen is unaffected by all the action and violence played upon it.

If you ask how mere watchfulness can change your inner structure, the best answer is to have the personal experience. But briefly, Silent Seeing detaches you from a false sense of self. You come to understand that these vagrant thoughts are not *you;* the essential *you* is something quite different. Along with this insight comes profound and delightful change.

HOW "SILENT SEEING" LEADS TO NEW HAPPINESS

Some people ask, "But why should I observe my inner turmoil? The awareness in itself is disturbing. I want to ignore the pain, not join it."

We cannot truly ignore anything until we are first aware of it. It is like having a slight headache. Unless I first pay attention to the fact of my headache, how can I intelligently deal with it? To ignore the pain is to perpetuate it. But my awareness of its existence leads to wise action.

Do you now see why the vast majority of people fail in their quest for newness? It is because they do not separate themselves from negative thoughts; they mistakenly take them as part of the basic self. But Silent Seeing changes things. It frees one of any kind of unwanted thought. It provides the ability to cut off these tormenting invaders the moment they appear, leaving one in peace.

Here is a summary for practicing the liberating art of Silent Seeing:

1. *Be aware of an arising thought.*

2. *Watch it silently, impersonally, unemotionally.*
3. *Call it neither good nor bad, right nor wrong.*
4. *Let it fade away of itself.*
5. *Practice your Silent Seeing moment by moment.*

Review these case histories connected with Silent Seeing:

1. Mrs. L. asked for a practical example of thought-watching, to which I replied, "Have you ever been at a noisy public gathering of some kind to find yourself wondering what on earth you were doing there? That is profitable thought-watching." She said the example was helpful, for she had found herself in such a situation.

2. Mr. F., a businessman, wanted to connect Silent Seeing with his business life. I advised him to watch what his mind was doing while he was taking time out for lunch. He got the point by reporting, "My body left the office but my mind remained at my cluttered desk. From now on I will relax at lunch."

3. Miss Y. wondered how the Silent Seeing of uncomfortable thoughts could lead to personal happiness. I told her, "We rise to a higher level of happiness only by seeing the pain of the present level. If a fireman does not first see a fire, how can he put it out?"

HOW EMOTIONAL SHOCKS CAN TURN INTO HAPPINESS

Authentic growth toward happiness comes by *taking shocks with awareness.* Let's see what this means.

When we are faced with an unwanted truth, we are shocked. If we resist the blow by repressing it or denying it, we cannot learn from it, in fact, we are worse off than before. But if we are aware of the blow, we can see its cause in the clash between what is true and what we falsely claim is true. Our willing exposure of our falseness wins release from its pain.

A man is called a hypocrite. He is shocked. Now, he is faced with a crisis. If he lies or denies, he cannot become aware of his hypocrisy, and therefore remains enslaved by it. But if he honestly goes through the painful shock of seeing his hypocrisy, if he lets his deceit rise to consciousness, he frees himself.

Everything depends upon whether we will bear the pain of self-exposure in order to be free and happy.

Here are helpful questions about happiness asked after one of my lectures:

Q. You speak a lot about the need to understand desire. Will you please explain how desire connects with happiness?

A. Getting what you want does not enrich your essence, therefore, it cannot increase happiness. But when denied what you want, and seeing it with understanding, you increase essence, which increases happiness. Your essence is happiness itself, so now you know where to work.

Q. I try to think happy thoughts, but nothing changes for the better. Why do I fail?

A. Because thoughts about happiness are not the same thing as happiness itself. Thinking about a bluebird does not make you a bluebird. Happiness reveals itself when the frantic mind ceases all its chasings and calculations.

Q. I know what will make me happy, but cannot attain it.

A. If you know what will make you happy, you don't know. If you know, you will be unhappy when what you desire fails to appear or goes away. But if you don't know what will make you happy, you are happy, because you have nothing to lose. To have no ideas whatsoever as to what will make you happy is happiness itself.

Q. I want so much to understand you, but doubt my ability.

A. Whatever is truly better for you is also truly possible for you. And since happiness is better than misery, happiness is possible.

TEN WAYS TO AWAKEN TO NEW HAPPINESS
FOR PERFECT LIVING

1. *Refuse trifles:* We waste our lives in trifles, not seeing them as such, because we prefer shallow self-entertainments. If you feel suddenly lost and empty, the exciting activity which preceded these feelings was a trifle.

2. *Think realistically toward money:* In the financial history of mankind, no man has ever feared a lack or loss of money. He has feared only his own fearful thoughts toward lack and loss. Your understanding of this has great power for peace.

3. *Drop self-labels:* Self-labels are self-imprisonments. If I call myself a leader of men or a spiritual person or a loving parent, I do so because I fear my own freedom from vanity supporting self-labels. I must learn to soar in the sky of my own free, unattached, undefined nature.

4. *Use unhappiness wisely:* A stab of pain indicates the presence of a false notion which must be made conscious. When unhappy, try to discover where some belief of yours contradicts a cosmic reality. Do not try to ignore pain, any more than you would ignore an irritating itch.

5. *Practice mental silence:* Instead of trying to activate cosmic powers within, we should remain silent in order to see them already at work. Make it your task for today not to try to achieve anything, but to quietly watch yourself being moved about by inner forces.

6. *Work for self-unity:* The less the distance between private thoughts and public behavior, the greater the happiness. Great relief can be won at once by ceasing to unconsciously ask, "Now, let's see, what is the proper facial expression for this occasion?"

7. *Bear uncertainty:* Every unhappy person has anxiously attached himself to useless beliefs, slogans and labels in an attempt to feel secure. But uncertainty, endured to the very end, destroys itself.

8. *Be truly independent:* Why should you care if no one misses you? You possess the capacity to be happy all by yourself. This does not mean to be anti-social; it means to live with the right person—your own mature self.

9. *Discover esotericism's great secrets:* When you know the great secrets, you can retire instantly. Genuine retirement has nothing to do with age or pensions. It is a mental retirement, where you live victoriously, retired from the world's follies.

10. *Cease to live in dreamland:* Dreamland, while promising bliss, delivers despair. There is something far above dreamland, of which you have not dreamed.

HOW DISCOURAGEMENT YIELDED TO RICHES

If I had to select an especially helpful kind of inquiry from seekers, it would be one like that of Gerald M. What a pleasure to discuss things with someone who does not understand, but deeply wishes to do so! Gerald stated, "I want to grasp esoteric principles, but am too discouraged over my life to make the necessary effort. Too many things have gone wrong, including family friction. I don't know what else to tell you, Mr. Howard, except that I'm totally discouraged."

"You do not understand," I told him. "Esotericism is *for* discouraged people—for the discouraged who *know* their discouragement. It cannot possibly be for anyone else. So you are in exactly the right state of mind."

His eyes took on a quizzical expression, as if requesting an explanation, so I continued, "Try to think in a new way toward what I am about to tell you, then it will become clear." He nodded.

"The last people on earth to study esotericism," I said, "are those filled with what they call confidence and wisdom. Why should they search for gold when their vanity informs them they already have it? Those who need the truth the most are the last to seek it. Because it is all a sham, such people are like flimsy scarecrows who fall apart at the slightest adverse breeze."

Gerald commented, "Of course. We see this all around. I once knew a man who was praised as a great intellectual and as a strong leader of men. When his wife left him, he turned into a sobbing alcoholic."

"Such a man must no longer believe in himself; that is, *he must be discouraged over his own lies about himself.* Only then is there true hope for him. You can place money only in an empty safe, not one cluttered with trash."

Gerald said with a nod, "That is my exact position."

"Good. Your very discouragement is your necessary space. You are ready to receive esoteric riches."

Gerald is a perfect example of how self-change begins with new understanding. He changed his life by the intelligent process of using his very discouragement as a starting point toward true happiness.

HOW HAPPINESS COMES ALL BY ITSELF

Happiness cannot be found by *trying*.

A group of passengers at an airport fell into a friendly discussion. Each volunteered to tell of a main source of his or her happiness. One man said he belonged to a large and famous business firm, which gave him a sense of purpose and importance. A woman smilingly said she belonged to her family, which was anxiously waiting for her at the end of her trip.

A third passenger happily told the others that his life belonged to a powerful political party which desperately needed his talents for winning the next election. Another woman eagerly said she belonged to a religious organization, and she was a vital part of its grand crusade to drive sin from the world.

A fifth passenger, who had remained silent, was asked about his source of happiness, to which he replied, "I've never belonged to anything, but I guess that's because I've never tried to be happy, I just *am* happy."

When we no longer try to be happy, happiness *is*. It comes to the whole person, to the self-discovered person.

You belong only to yourself, to your own essence. Man's misery comes from vain attempts to lodge elsewhere. *"What do you suppose will satisfy the soul, except to walk free and own no superior?"* (Walt Whitman)

Bert H. asked the following questions:

> **Q.** I have a suspicion of the wrongness of my life, but cannot see any alternative. For example, how can I be happy without having what is called worldly success?
>
> **A.** Motorists may feel sorry for the solitary wanderer sitting by the side of the road with all his worldly goods on his back, but perhaps he is the only one who doesn't know that he is unhappy. He may have insights which make him feel sorry for the poor motorists trapped by society's stupid obsessions.

Q. I cannot tell the difference between what is right and what is wrong, which makes my mind a whirlwind. There are thousands of contradictory opinions about morality. What can we do?

A. A false society has imposed upon you a false conscience which chains down your natural happiness. By rising above society's falseness with trueness to your own nature, artificial conscience can neither exist nor pain you. True conscience springs from your recovered essence, and is the same for all who live from essence.

Q. I am tired of trying to figure out my duties toward society. The conflict is wearing me out.

A. Thank heaven for the day when you must choose between what you solemnly assume is your social duty and your wish to run out and play—and you choose to play.

WHAT PEOPLE FAIL TO REALIZE ABOUT THEIR MINDS

We awaken new feelings of happiness as we shed our own light upon our own minds. This is a happy idea in itself, for it means we can stop working in the dark and begin to see what we are doing to ourselves at every moment.

There exists in India a tall and ancient temple, overgrown with vines. When entering at the ground level you stand in dimness, but as you climb the steps to the top, you find yourself in sunlight. In life, you are both the temple and the light, so everything depends upon the part you occupy within yourself. I assure you that the steps are there and ready for you.

People simply do not realize what they say when complaining, "I am crushed by my debts and my bad marriage and my irritating conditions." They fail to realize that something can always be done with their *thinking* toward such human conditions. As if faulty conditions can exist outside a faulty mind!

If you do not paint a box black, can it be black? If the mind did not project its own painful labeling onto a condition, can it be painful? A man may object, "But you still can't deny my mountain of debts." But he cannot deny that the pain is still in his mind, and that it started with his own painful mental concept which he verbalizes as "debts." What are "debts"? Can you eat them, ride them, put them in your pocket? Can they attack you, bite you? Of course not. They are human-level ideas only, and are connected with a wrong idea a man has about himself—that he is now a "failure" because of his "debts."

"Debts" exist only because society has agreed to call a certain financial condition by that name. It is therefore only a human-level *word*, but people painfully react to the word as if it were real, and as if it had power to cause pain. They react to acquired mental associations, not to realities. A free mind is above human-level labeling, and therefore in command of it. This means it can experience, if necessary, the human-level condition called "debts" without personal distress. It must also be remembered that going deeply into debt itself can usually be traced to faulty thinking.

We must realize that human-level thinking cannot solve human-level problems, any more than we can fly in an automobile. But happily, esoteric thinking is an aircraft capable of flight above earthly disorder.

When any kind of unhappiness appears, ask over and over, "Where does this pain really exist?" Continue with this until you see something you never saw before.

REVIEW THESE IDEAS ABOUT HAPPINESS

1. Happiness and mental clarity are the very same thing.
2. Let esoteric wisdom offer its quietness to you.
3. The wolves of the mind can be banished forever.
4. Practice the liberating art of Silent Seeing.
5. Shocks taken with awareness lead to self-release.
6. Discover extraordinary secrets every day.
7. Psychic symbolism is a great help for discouraged people.
8. As we stop wrong efforts, happiness *comes by itself*.
9. Let your own mind shed light on yourself.
10. Right thinking provides a new kind of permanent happiness.

9

How to Let Yourself
Be Carried by
Life's Easy Flow

If you wish an esoterically correct and highly practical definition of true living, call it an *Easy Flow*.

Once you see what this means, your day will never be the same. The purpose of this chapter is to change your day into an Easy Flow. It is immensely important that you do not take the term Easy Flow as something merely poetic or philosophical, for that is the last thing it is. It is practical, workable, something the businessman at his desk or the homemaker at her stove can use for moment-by-moment ease and pleasantness.

How to Overcome the Force of Daily Frustrations

First of all, we must review how the average man goes through his day. Your own observation reveals how he struggles tensely with unexpected crises, and how he nervously fights the frustration of his desires. He is painfully and constantly faced with things he feels he must either attack or avoid. He anxiously wishes to be somewhere else doing something else, but never knows what. No matter how hard he tries to win the pleasurable and avoid the painful, he alternates monotonously between the two and, sadly, his hoped for solutions merely degenerate into new problems. Obviously, he is not living within the Easy Flow of life; he is not a happy man, but a hounded man.

Using the simplest of terms, let's see what is meant by living with Easy Flow.

It means to meet every event with a fresh and unconditioned mind, without all the anger and distress of the average man.

It means to have no stubborn notions of how other people should treat you, thus allowing freedom, flexibility and happiness, no matter how you are treated.

It means to refuse to be jolted out of your Easy Flow by intruding thoughts which try to accuse and agitate you, and make you miserable.

Finally, it means to live lightly from your own spontaneous essence, from which flows authentic wisdom and peace.

Declare with Walt Whitman:

> **From this hour I ordain myself loos'd of limits and imaginary lines,**
> **Going where I list, my own master, total and absolute . . .**

HOW A BOAT TRIP WAS HANDLED WITH EASY FLOW

A man who owned a boat wanted to take a trip down a river. But knowing nothing about such a trip, he consulted those who claimed expertness on river travel. He was surprised to find so many of them. Paying their fees, he collected all sorts of theories and opinions. It took him time to sort out the bewildering information, for the experts were quite vague, and often contradicted each other.

But out of the maze of advice, he mapped out a definite plan for traveling down the river, as follows: During stormy weather, he would take shelter at various coves along the riverbank. As a landmark, he would use a point where the river made a bend to the west. He would rest from time to time by taking naps while in smooth waters.

On paper, everything looked just fine. So with high hopes, he boarded his boat and headed downstream.

Troubles arose at once. A storm came up, but the coves he had counted upon were non-existent. Worry overcame him when the river turned to the east, not west. So unexpectedly rough were the waters that he was too nervous to rest. Nothing happened according to plan.

He suffered intensely—that is, until he made a magnificent discovery.

The river itself was not causing his disturbance, instead, it was his preconceived belief as to what it should be like.

This led to a second amazing revelation.

By abandoning his fixed ideas as to how the river should flow, he could flow along with it, easily, effortlessly, untroubled.

So setting aside his fixed plans, he glided happily forward.

The wondrous Easy Flow has been presented to mankind by all the authentic teachers and teachings. They explain it in different terms, but all mean the same thing. The New Testament calls it the Kingdom of Heaven within. Shankara, the ancient mystic, spoke of it as Oneness of the self with the universe. Plato simply referred to it as freedom from dark thoughts.

In summary, a man can live from his false center, which is misery, or from his Easy Flow within, which is total restfulness and fulfillment. The choice is his own. You belong within the Easy Flow. Let yourself be where you belong.

YOU NEED NOT BE TRAPPED BY FORCED LIVING

In the absence of Easy Flow, what do we have? We have Forced Living. Glance around at the tragic human drama. What do you see? A thousand varieties of Forced Living. Look at that pitiful man, struggling to win attention and admiration, while vaguely sensing the folly of it all. Look at that woman, squandering her life in a frantic attempt to find security by close attachment to family and friends, and seething with secret hostility toward all who oppose her. Look at that mob of nervous and frightened people, gathered together to advance what they call a noble cause, anxiously hoping that the noise of their own confusion will somehow drown out the awful scream of their inner torture.

Forced Living arises from the artificial self, consequently, it is unnatural, strained, dishonest, demanding, rude and it never stops talking. It is terrified that its little scheme will fall apart.

It has no conscience whatsoever, though it is quite clever in masquerading as love.

How Nancy's Life Became Her Own

Nancy B. suffered from one form of Forced Living. She felt compelled to fall in line with what others suggested. So she often found herself in places where she really did not want to be, doing things of no real interest to her. Sensing that her constant consent was costing her time, energy and even money, she wanted to call a halt to her admitted gullibility, but did not know where to start.

As we talked things over, Nancy changed everything by simply understanding what was going on. She was told that her first mistake was the abandonment of her own natural intelligence to the shallow and often selfish ideas of others. Secondly, she was told about her dormant ability to do what was best for *herself,* for her true interests. She was advised not to be afraid to be without the so-called excitements to which she was invited. In this regard she was asked to observe the concealed unhappiness of the friends who appeared to be so gay on the surface. Finally, Nancy was advised to begin a reading program of esoteric books, which would expand both her self-knowledge and her daily independence.

As Nancy worked, she nicely proved things for herself. Her life became her own; she no longer hesitated to say *no* to invitations which had no appeal for her. She lived within the Easy Flow.

If you, like Nancy, feel that you are trapped by Forced Living, you can also use esoteric truths to live in a totally new way— within the Easy Flow.

HOW TO AWAKEN TO YOUR COSMIC RICHES

The contrasting lives of two famous teachers show the difference between Forced Living and Easy Flow.

Confucius was an advocate of correct public behavior. He

taught good manners, social reform, and submission to man-made moral codes. He offered shallow formulas for getting through life, admitting that his platitudes were borrowed from other men. The inner life of cosmic peace was unknown to Confucius; he himself was a victim of Forced Living.

Lao-tse was the exact opposite. He cared nothing for the public parading of self-proclaimed virtues. He pointed out that human rules of conduct do not make men truly moral; to the contrary, they supply clever masks for hypocrisy and cruelty. As for living by popular slogans, they create mass misery and national neurosis. Lao-tse stressed individual effort toward personal freedom, teaching that happiness lies in a spontaneous outflowing of one's natural self. Lao-tse was himself a living example of Easy Flow.

Confucius was in his thirties when he visited Lao-tse, then a sage in his eighties. We might picture what the wise man said to the young inquirer. For one thing, Lao-tse might have pointed out that human reformers never seek justice for their followers; they wish only to grasp the power of injustice for themselves. He might also have said that a formal education does not mean intelligence, for true intelligence is to live within the spontaneous rhythm of life, without cunning and deceit, and with sanity and naturalness.

Lao-tse was a teacher of Taoism. In your march toward the superior way, you may wish to investigate Taoist literature.

What is true intelligence? For one thing, it is to see material things from the cosmic viewpoint. This viewpoint shows how material items arise from cosmic sources. Such intelligence provides freedom from worry over money and other physical possessions. Once we understand that money must be used only for the support of life on the physical level and not for unconscious ego-gratification, all anxiety toward money falls away forever.

Do not worry about being left out of the good things of life. Do not feel badly about it. With cosmic awakening, you will see that you are not left out and never were. What you used to consider valuable is now seen as worthless, and what you formerly ignored, you now treasure.

If you place the wish for relief before the wish for understanding, you will have neither genuine relief nor understanding. But if you set the desire for understanding before the wish for relief, you will have both true relief and understanding.

Esoteric truths speak directly to the intuitive self of whoever is receptive to them.

THREE PRACTICAL PRINCIPLES FOR NEW INSIGHTS

A Louisiana woman wrote to tell me that her biggest problem was resentment toward unexpected events. She went to work with the very same principles which you are now covering in this book. Her negativities fell away, releasing her to new heights of insight and happiness. Her bright success resulted from three procedures, which will also work for you: (1) Be willing to learn new methods. (2) Seek out accurate sources of guidance. (3) Prefer inner authentic happiness to a mere public display of feigned happiness.

Let the following questions turn on more light:

Q. Is it hard work to grasp these principles?

A. You have a choice of either thinking rightly or wrongly. I guarantee that it is a thousand times harder to think wrongly than rightly. You prove this every moment. Try to see the necessity of right thinking.

Q. Please explain personal effort.

A. Right effort must be made, but when enlightenment dawns, its nature changes. It takes personal effort to reach personal effortlessness. You must row your boat from the river's edge to its center, after which the boat is carried forward by the river.

Q. You have urged us to use our relations with other people to gain self-insight. How can I start?

A. By not seeing others according to your personal needs. Do not assume that others are wise or strong, for you will merely be seeing them as you want them to be. This leads to disillusionment. All this means you must first detect your own false needs.

Q. How can I tell whether an action of mine is performed from my own harmful self-will, or whether it arises from the Easy Flow of life?

A. There are several clues. Actions from self-will start with anxiety and confusion and are kept going by shaky hopes and worried expectations. They conclude with disappointment, or in emotional elation which gives way to emptiness. By observing your negative motivations, you weaken them, making way for the Easy Flow.

HOW TO LET GO TO ENTER THE EASY FLOW

We come now to the supreme question: How do we enter the Easy Flow, in which all is wonderfully different?

We can examine the classical teachings, for they all agree in essence, though providing various methods:

> Socrates: *"Get rid of unconscious delusions."*
> Epictetus: *"Let life lead you in its own right way."*
> Sufism: *"Find union with the Divine."*
> Baruch Spinoza: *"Surrender the passions."*
> Hinduism: *"Extinguish the ego."*
> Ralph Waldo Emerson: *"Don't conform to sick society."*
> William Blake: *"See beyond yourself."*
> Zen: *"Let go!"*

Let go of *what*? It means, finally, to let go of the great pretense that we know what we are doing with our lives. It means to let go of the assumption that head-knowledge is the same as esoteric insight. It means to release pride and vanity, to abandon shallow traditions that only seem to offer support.

Beyond the release of ourselves, we find ourselves in our true identity. The process of ego-release can only be accomplished with small steps at any one time; otherwise, it is too shocking and frightening. But even small courage can result in small success, which builds more courage for the next and larger success. Novelist Fyodor Dostoyevsky, who had insight into these things, once remarked that we are required to understand only what we can at the moment, not what we cannot.

Let's see how the practice of self-release can aid you in a practical, everyday situation. When you don't know how to behave in a forthcoming event, why do you think about it at all? Why not let go of your hastily made plans? Your plans consist merely of ideas which you assume may protect you or deliver a gain of some kind. But this prevents spontaneous action which can handle each arising challenge with ease and accuracy. Banish the ego and you banish the crisis, for the crisis is in the ego, though it appears to be in the situation. (This is also an example of the esoteric teaching about non-action, which is true action.)

This is the sort of practice that really changes you. Can you sense this? Let go of the old, for that alone can create the new.

HOW TO ELIMINATE YOUR OBSTRUCTIONS TO EASY FLOW

What obstructs our entrance into the peace of Easy Flow? As always, we come back to the primary problem of man—his dreadful capacity to live in false ideas about himself. *Man refuses to enter Easy Flow because he fearfully senses that it means the loss of what he calls his "individuality." But this ridiculous "individuality" is the very cause of all his misery and frustration. However, because he refuses to see this, he clings desperately to the very illusion that destroys him.* This is why the throne is attained only by the courageous, by those who demand no guarantees, who do not reach out with one hand while clinging with the other.

Reach out! Within your grasp is that which you have secretly yearned for all your life. Do not be afraid, for there is nothing to fear; there is only something amazingly beautiful.

You now understand this on the intellectual level. Go on to the total experience.

How to Eliminate Anxieties and Depressions

A retired army officer once wrote to me, admitting his inability to handle retirement. He felt restless, insecure, believed himself to be a failure. While used to successful command in military life, he was dismayed to find an absence of self-command in his new circumstances. He felt that he must try to force his life forward, but at the same time he sensed the futility of trying to force things. We discussed basic solutions from the esoteric viewpoint, which can work for you as well as it did for him. Let's cover a few.

The reason we anxiously push life in general and a project in particular is because we fear, falsely, that things may stop. We fear the stopping of an activity because we fear we may stop with it, being left empty and without purpose. But the very pursuit of a particular activity is futility itself; nothing can come of it except further anxiety. It is chasing our shadow.

To make this quite clear, I want to explain an esoteric principle of immense importance to you. Because it is new to you, it may appear puzzling, so persist in your attempt to grasp its value.

A man, of himself, does not *do* anything. He is a follower of events, not their creator. When he succeeds in an outer ambition, it merely means he has fallen in line with a chain of events that happened to coincide with his ambition. So the success is not really his own, and neither would his failure be. Failure merely indicates that his ambition and the event did not coincide.

Do you see why this is a liberating factor? It means liberty from all our anxiety toward success and our depression toward failure. It means that we remain in perfect peace, no matter what reality hands us. It can be compared with the sun which remains constant in the sky, regardless of stormy weather on earth.

HOW TO SUCCEED WITH EVERY DAILY EVENT

Life moves us; we do not move life. When we learn how to follow events intelligently, rather than try to create them, we have cracked open a great mystery, which is unsolved by the vast majority of men and women on earth. No, this does not mean the surrender of individuality or of private intelligence. It means finding them for the first time. It means a new and kingly kind of thinking, which flows freely and with pleasure.

Ralph K. opened the consultation with, "You have made me at least dimly aware of my faulty responses to disappointing events. I sense the futility of meeting them with annoyance or dismay. Could we explore it further, please?"

We can go into Ralph's problem together with considerable

profit, for our reactions to daily challenges make our day one of defeat or one of victory.

Suppose a man knew only five words of his language, perhaps *hello, yes, no, today, tomorrow.* Walking down the street, a friend asks him, "How are you?" to which he replies, "No." Another person asks him for the time of day, to which he responds, "Tomorrow."

That man's response is faulty; it makes no sense. And since these are the only responses he knows, he cannot possibly meet life with skill, no matter how hard he tries.

Now, this is how most men and women respond inadequately to their hundreds of daily challenges. And it is exactly why the day goes so badly. A fixed, often negative, old mind cannot handle the new. It is like trying to understand today's news stories with last week's newspaper. The mind must function with moment-by-moment newness. We achieve this by daring to let go of hardened thinking habits which masquerade as intelligence.

Here is a man who has developed the reaction of envy, of which he is unaware. He meets someone with more money or prestige or leisure time. Inwardly, he compares himself with the other, and envy arises, accompanied by painful hostility. Here is a woman who has permitted bitterness toward men to warp her mind. Because she cannot see her faulty mental habit, bitterness creeps into her relationships with men, robbing her of happiness.

We must become aware of our mechanical reactions, for that awareness cracks the painful pattern and sets us free.

HOW TO ABANDON SELF-REFERENCE IN DAILY EVENTS

One way to break free is to consistently abandon self-reference. Meet daily events without connecting them with your personal interests. It may seem impossible to do this, for you wonder how anything can be met without self-interest. I assure you that here is one of the great secrets of the ages. Try to get the feeling of *I* and *me* and *mine* out of occurrences.

The question may arise, "Why all this attention to self-understanding, rather than attending to exterior matters, like family problems and political confusions?"

Because a man somehow senses that there is something wrong with himself; this causes human conflicts. Even if we refuse to face it, we know that our problems arise from within ourselves. So self-inquiry is the only honest and intelligent course to take. *"In other living creatures, ignorance of self is nature; in man it is vice."* (Boethius)

Isabel C. and I discussed this as follows:

Q. Please explain the cause and cure of tension.

A. First of all, remember that mental, emotional and physical tension are connected. If one relaxes, so do the others. A basic cause of tension and pressure is a fear of letting go. One falsely feels that abandonment of his opinions and efforts will cause a disastrous disintegration of his life.

Q. You mean we fear the very relaxation we seek?

A. Exactly. You falsely assume that tension is a power which keeps your life together; therefore, you must also falsely assume that relaxation will destroy it. To dissolve this dangerous delusion, you must let go, in spite of your hesitations.

Q. But it is so difficult!

A. Do two things. First, stand aside and observe your nervous pursuit of life. This acquaints you with your frantic chasings, which you now do unconsciously. Next, with quiet decision, let your day flow forward in any way it likes, without concern for what happens to you. This will reveal the existence within you of a place which cannot be touched by anything.

Q. It really works?

A. I assure you that it is the only thing that does.

WHY EVERYTHING BECOMES DIFFERENT WITHIN THE EASY FLOW

At the start of this chapter I advised that these principles be taken as entirely practical. I did this because I know how easy it is to dismiss esoteric teachings as being too remote for daily practice and benefit. So now I want to show you how one woman worked her way toward Easy Flow. Before understanding these ideas, one of her problems was stated like this: "My boss drives me mad with his orders to do a half dozen things at once; he accuses and blames me for things he does himself."

She no longer wanted to be involved in this nerve-shaking situation, but also knew that quitting her employment was no solution. What, then, could she do? Searching around for aid, she soon realized that no one else had the answer. Finally, she came into contact with esoteric teachings, which gave her a sense of something entirely new. She had the feeling, rather than the thought, that before her stretched a vast psychic country where everything was fantastically different. From esoteric books and lectures she picked up basic gems of insight, like these:

1. *There is a totally new way to meet daily life.*
2. *My old concepts must vanish entirely.*
3. *I must place psychic awakening before all else.*
4. *My pain arises from lack of cosmic understanding.*
5. *I must willingly receive the newness offered.*

Her new insights led to new victories, expressed in these words: "I observe now that he wanted me to get panicky because this gave him a feeling of power, and I also see that his internal chaos need have no bearing on me."

There is something whispering to you at every moment, whether in home or office, in both success and failure, regardless of age and environment and background. It is the faint but persistent whisper that *everything can be different.*

Listen, and you can hear it right now, at this very moment, even while you hold this book.

Listen quietly, attentively. With mental and physical relaxation, listen to what it is trying to tell you, for it is good news. "*A man should learn to detect and watch that gleam of light which flashes across his mind from within. . . .*" (Ralph Waldo Emerson)

It is trying to tell you of great sleeping powers for self-deliverance, which you must awaken and put to use. It urges you not to be afraid of losing certain friends and dreams and ambitions, whose familiarity gives the painful illusion of security. It repeats over and over that cosmic self-command is reached by first shattering the human pretense of self-command. It assures that the

forces in your favor can overwhelm completely all those opposi-
tions which appear so menacing.

Begin at once to apply these principles to your daily actions,
for that is how life becomes an Easy Flow.

VALUABLE POINTS FOR YOUR REFLECTION

1. The life of Easy Flow can be yours.
2. Rightly met, daily events become rich discoveries.
3. Nothing on earth has power to trap you to your detriment.
4. Fall in with the spontaneous flow of your nature.
5. Be receptive to your inner whisperings of truth.
6. Let go!
7. There is no need to fear anything whatsoever.
8. Use these ideas to succeed with every daily event.
9. Self-inquiry opens the door to fresh experiences.
10. When resting within the Easy Flow, every day is new.

10

The Mystic Cure
for Worry and Tension
in Your Life

You may have hopefully counted on that marriage or that involvement or that success to cover up the awful ache inside you. But they failed you, as they always must, leaving you confused and afraid. And now, since you do not know what to do next, the dreadful pain has gone underground.

In your weary search, you listened to so many authorities with a reputation for knowing the answers. But you could tell by the vague look in their eyes and by their forceful dramatics that they were working too hard to really know. You began to think it was easier when you used to deceive yourself; when you sought comfort by quoting wise sayings which you never really understood. But with some anxiety you realize you can never go back; you can no longer accept stones as bread.

And having taken that step, a new terror looms ahead. Having cut off your retreat, what lies ahead? What if there is nothing there? What if you are all alone and lost?

There is good news. There is something out there. You can find it. No, it will not be easy at first, but that is only because you are going against the stubborn habits of the years. They can be broken. Just employ whatever courage and persistence you have, even if only an ounce, and they will strengthen you.

The great Source of the faint whisper you now hear can be found. That is what you must keep in mind always. It can be found. So set your face in the direction of that whisper and walk on.

HOW TO ABOLISH YOUR LIFE'S TROUBLES

There is a magical way to abolish your life's troubles. That sure way is not to mind them when they come. This does not mean a pretense of indifference to daily challenges; it means to destroy their false power with clear wisdom. It is like a terrified savage who finds himself imprisoned in a circle of fierce-looking, wooden idols. He dares to push them over, which exposes the green hills beyond.

You have asked yourself a thousand times, "Is there no answer to this awful, secret nagging that persists wherever I go and whatever I do?"

Yes, there is an answer, but it cannot be caught in the ponds in which you have been fishing till now. You have not caught it for two reasons. (1) You have not preferred the answer over your fixed ideas of what is right. (2) You have not known what to do about your secretly unhappy state.

Let's follow one person's worries and tensions through to a happy ending.

"I sometimes wonder," Shirley C. told me with a tired voice, "whether love between a man and a woman really exists. So much that is not love parades around as that virtue." She went on to tell me about her several love affairs with men, all ending in heartache. All of them started out with moonlight and roses, she said, giving promise of shared happiness. But sooner or later they degenerated into petty quarreling and finally into separation.

"I want so badly to love someone and to be loved by him," she said, "that I'll sacrifice almost anything for it. I need a nice man. If the weekends get any lonelier, I won't be able to go on." She tried hard to hold back the tears, which finally fell.

I knew the difficulties Shirley faced in trying to grasp the help I had for her. I realized the resistances and misinterpretations she would make when I presented esoteric solutions. I also knew she would react, as people always do, by wondering why I had strayed so far from her immediate problem. Still wrongly assuming that the addition of a man would cure her loneliness, she would be puzzled when I talked about ideas far removed from that subject.

But we had to start somewhere, so I gave Shirley some basic principles which could help her to the exact degree of her receptivity. The following ideas are a summary of what I told her.

A REFRESHING WAY TO LOOK AT SUCCESS

The only answer to any worry or tension is self-knowledge. To think that the answer exists in any exterior acquisition will only lead to a repetition of the pain—as Shirley discovered. Shankara, the Eastern wise man, provided a good illustration of using wrong methods. He compared it with crossing a river on a crocodile, while mistaking it for a log. No wonder everyone is uneasy.

Not having enough self-insight at this point, Shirley had fallen into several traps. One of them was to use the word "love" in a situation barren of that virtue. Until we learn the true meaning of love, we must not even use the word, for it is a type of self-deception.

Also, Shirley must not confuse love with dependency. To the exact degree that we are dependent upon another, we will be unconsciously hostile toward him. Hero-worship always includes its opposite, and the slightest lapse on the part of the idol will turn the so-called love to hate. Esoterically, love exists when we are free of the need to use another for any type of self-gratification.

In conclusion, I pointed out to Shirley, "You are presently motivated by memories of past pleasures with men. The driving desire for their repetition blocks out your awareness of immaturity in both you and the man. Not wanting to see your own weaknesses, you fail to see the very same negativities in the man. So you walk straight into each other's trap. Study yourself. Be aware of your compulsive need for excitement, for pseudo-pleasure, based on memories of past pleasures. Be a new person today. That will change the pattern. You will no longer be the unconscious and unwilling slave of your own pain."

Shirley called me long-distance several weeks later to say, "I could not grasp what you said at the time, but I could not keep your words out of my mind. It is really strange how it happened, like small seeds breaking apart to push above ground as young plants. May I talk with you again?"

There is a way to be successful every day. It is to determine that each worry or tension will reveal some new esoteric secret to you. Then, no event can be called a failure, for you are succeeding inwardly, *which is the only place that counts.*

Instead of complaining about a disappointing event, you study why you felt disappointed. Is that not success? Rather than allowing another's unkind remark to make you angry, you see that nothing can hurt you without your consent. Is that not success? Look at success in this refreshing way.

HOW TO ACQUIRE VISION FOR NEW INSIGHTS

Imagine a soldier who has just been captured by an enemy squad. His captors believe he may have valuable military information, so they devise a plan to make him talk. After blindfolding him, they march him around for awhile in several directions. Brought to a halt, he is told that he stands at the very edge of a dangerous cliff. Hinting that the very worst will happen unless he talks, they demand information.

The prisoner is, of course, frightened and helpless. His mind races around for possible escapes. Maybe they would believe false information. Perhaps he can appeal to their mercy. Help may come from his own army. But no matter what he thinks about, his desperation remains. There seems to be no escape.

Suddenly, a surprise occurs. Ever so little, the blindfold slips aside, exposing a tiny section of the outside world. Unnoticed by his captors, the prisoner catches glimpses of things as they really are. For one thing, he notices that the soldiers are grinning pleasantly at each other. Also, he sees he is nowhere near a cliff, but in a colorful meadow.

Realization comes to him. The soldiers are not serious. They mean him no harm. It is all a game. With this, his tension falls away. He no longer seeks a way out. He knows he is already out, and always was.

If only we will look! If only we will see! Here are four glimpses which can set you free.

1. You must not resent the attempts of others to drain your psychic energy. Be aware of their attempts to do so, realizing it is characteristic of everyone living in the unnatural world. Those on a low level of understanding cannot see any other way to exist than at the expense of others. But you must be on the higher level, where you do not unconsciously resist this evil, but are free of it. You achieve this by being a man or a woman who *sees*.

2. There is much work to be done if you still think that others should behave in the way that pleases you. They cannot and they will not do so, nor is it necessary as far as your wholeness is concerned. You must allow people and events to act as they must, according to their own level, and not according to your desires. Faithful practice of this will destroy self-contradictions and deliver happiness.

3. When a man no longer has a need for psychic sickness, it falls away, making him healthy. Man, in his present state, delights in sickness. Why? If the sick Mr. A can find something wrong with the sick Mr. B, Mr. A falsely thinks he has relieved his own guilt. Also, how can Mr. A see himself as a good man unless he can compare himself with the bad Mr. B? Besides, what a great opportunity to go onstage as the compassionate teacher and healer of the pitiful Mr. B! A truly healthy man is aware of human sickness, but has no need to exploit it.

4. You cannot live comfortably in any world you laboriously create for yourself; it will battle you day and night, leaving you tired and agitated. But if you do not try to build your own world, if you cease anxious effort, an entirely new world presents itself to you. In this new world there is no separation between you and it; you are One with it. There is no self who needs to direct and control the affairs of this astonishing world; there is only total control, of which you are a comfortable part.

HOW TO ENVISION YOUR NEW SELF

Will you begin to see uncomfortable things with the eyes of esoteric insight, and so banish them? Start today to do so. Take mental and emotional strain, which induces physical tension. Can you quietly observe the strain of trying to influence people and events according to your desires? Can you see the burden of compulsive thoughts, which make you weary? Can you notice the nervousness in hoping for something good to happen?

You can glimpse a new self by impersonally watching yourself being moved about during your day. Just be a passive observer of the movements of mind, feelings, body. Do this in place of thinking that you are moving yourself about. As the East Indian teacher, Sri Ramana Maharshi, has pointed out, man's whole problem consists in the illusion that he is the doer, instead of the follower. It is the Higher Power which moves everything.

Someday you will see that life itself imposes no strain on you. Strain exists in the gap between what we *insist we need* and what we *actually receive*. Destroy the *insistence* and you destroy the gap and the pain.

So it is certain that strained effort is all wrong. There is something in you quite capable of effort without strain. It is like the enjoyable effort made when learning to paint a picture. Life fails to flow freely because we try to *make* it flow. What would you think of a man who tried to make a river flow forward in order to carry him? That man has deluded himself into thinking he is the doer, when he need only rest and let the river carry him forward.

This explanation led to questions from Everett L.:

Q. At one time you said that we must take charge of our lives, yet another time you urged us to abandon our efforts. Please explain.

A. Take charge by abandoning the false notion that you are now in charge. When you are truly in charge you don't have headaches and hostilities. Right effort is to abandon useless effort based in ignorance of psychic facts.

Q. How can we handle worries and frustrations in business affairs?

A. Worries disappear when you conduct your business to earn a living, but not to picture yourself as a success. Because you no longer think in the opposite terms of success and failure, neither riches nor poverty can affect you.

Q. But all of us have this terribly compulsive need to be a winner, to be valuable.

A. You need not be valuable. You need only realize your capacity to receive the valuable.

HOW TO DISSOLVE FIFTEEN PAINFUL FEARS

Once I sat alongside a group of nervous and frightened people. Their facial expressions revealed inward anxiety. What bothered them? They were timidly waiting to take tests for a driver's license. Unfortunately, they were not on the esoteric path, which meant they were unaware of their fright. They were *one* with their fears, and so could not stand aside to study them.

This is certain: man is enslaved by fear. Let's take fifteen common anxieties and then apply a new cure. But do not be like those about to take the driver's test; instead, be alert to what is going on within yourself. As you read the following list, be aware of your own reactions, for that is healthy self-awareness. A man fears:

Displeasing other people
Helplessness before the future
Not knowing who he is
His own weakness and folly
Absence of excitement and stimulation
Exposure of his insincerity and pretense
Unexpected financial expenses
Punishment from God
Being unnoticed and unwanted
His suppressed hatreds and cruelties
Being cheated and left out of things
Aloneness and loneliness
Raging fleshly appetites
Inability to change himself
Government power and public authorities

Fear is caused by attachments to fixed mental and emotional positions. It is the threat to these positions which makes us anxious and hostile. Now, every fixed position has an opposite which threatens to overthrow it at any time, which keeps us tense and nervous. If we desperately need things that are familiar, we fear the unknown. If we desire money, we fear its opposite, the loss of money. If we need society, we fear solitude. But a free mind, having no attachments, having nothing to lose, fears nothing.

This is exactly what the New Testament and other spiritual texts mean by being "poor in spirit." It means to be without the "riches" of psychological attachments. Try to separate a "rich" man from his public fame or his reputation for wisdom and he turns fearfully hostile. Do you know such a person?

HOW YOU CAN BE IMMUNE FROM FEAR

One of the sunniest facts ever to brighten your day is this: Since there is only one basic fear, there need be only one simple cure. That cure is to live according to your free and unattached nature. It is like a single washing of a jacket which cleans a dozen spots.

"Thank heaven," exclaimed Mildred G., "I heard your lecture on the need for dropping our pretenses. Unless you had pointed it out, I would never have believed how enslaved I am. I recently observed my resentment over having to use my postage stamp, because I thought another person should have used his stamp. But I pretended I didn't care. I now see that self-honesty, though shocking at first, brings great relief. I will work hard on myself from now on!"

Mildred was wisely freeing herself from the sixth fear on the preceding list, which can be illustrated like this: An actor is rehearsing a scene in an old theater so shaky it threatens to collapse upon his head at any moment. Though he pretends to be confident, he nervously forgets his lines and glances anxiously around. But if he stops acting, if he gets out of the theater, what is there to fear? Likewise, human fear ends when pretense ends.

Do we fear our own foolishness?

Unless we are willing to be consciously foolish, which would destroy foolishness, we will remain unconsciously foolish, which will preserve it.

Do unexpected events disturb us?

We should prefer a disturbing situation over a comfortable one, for we can learn from disturbance, but not from comfort which makes us too lazy to see the predicament we are bringing about.

Does the uncertain future make you apprehensive?

Don't you see that it is this present moment which you must set free, for what other moment is there?

Are you worried over your failure to shape your life?

You cannot lead life; you can only follow it, but that wise following is the true victory you want and need.

Are we confused over the endless conflicts in our day?

Whenever we are in conflict with either ourselves or others, it is because of something within us that will not admit it does not know what is right.

Do you fear those who seem to have power over you?

Once you understand your true nature, you will be immune to fear of anyone or anything.

LET GOOD THINGS COME TO YOU

It is time to get tired of it all. It is time to get utterly tired of being afraid of our inner emptiness, of anxiously waiting for good things to happen, of nervously hiding our defects from ourselves and others.

It is time to revolt. Not against social conditions or a cruel person in your life or against some frightening phantom in your financial affairs. That kind of revolt will only wear you out, for it is directed against the wrong enemy. The only enemy—note well—is your own wrong way of thinking.

It is time to take charge of your own life. Never mind if you have feelings of weakness or uncertainty. Such feelings are false, arising from wrong thoughts which you do not as yet see as wrong. Take charge of your life in the right way, and weakness disappears of itself, for it has no real support.

There is *your* answer to life's challenges, and there is *the* answer. If you will get out of your own way, what will become apparent?

Let me explain one type of fear which prevents inner advancement. It is the fear of not knowing what to do with yourself after reality has relieved you of useless activities. You see, that is what truth seeks to do—to take away pointless and self-harming activities, both mental and physical. Since you identify with these activities, since they give false values which you think are real, you resist their destruction.

The way to break through is to bear the pain. There is a pain-gap between the destruction of the old and the revelation of the new. The pain has a false foundation, but you cannot see this until you come out on the other side of the dark tunnel. So choose the pain and you will lose the pain; however, your motive must be to fully experience the pain, not to lose it.

Anyone can get a False Feeling of Life by involvement in activities requiring a stimulating response. But to live without inventing activities, and to respond correctly when there is no stimulation—that is true living.

You need not pursue anything whatsoever. All that is truly good for you will come your way effortlessly, once you realize the nature of the truly good. You need not pursue anything, for there is nothing needing pursuit; it is already in the here and now, needing only your realization. What you must realize is that the truly good is first invisible, after which it expresses itself in the visible.

Need an eagle pursue the sky in which it soars?

HOW TO GAIN NEW ENERGY

Keith C., a businessman who complained of unnatural tiredness and lack of energy, asked for the esoteric viewpoint on his problem. I supplied the following working ideas, which you can certainly adopt for your own benefit.

Tiredness arises from compulsively doing things which life has not asked us to do. The man who lives apart from his true nature is enslaved by both his own compulsive desires and his exterior pressures. He rises and falls with every passing influence, just as a thermometer mechanically obeys the dictates of the weather. So he remains resentful and worn out, not realizing the existence of a totally new way.

What kind of unrequired things drain a man? The list is an endless one of mental, emotional, physical and psychic drainage. He chatters when he has nothing to say. He anxiously feels the need to impress someone. He worries over the possible loss of someone important in his life. He thinks he must appear intelligent. He foolishly thinks it a good thing to have power over others.

What tragedy! What a waste of life! If he would courageously dare to do without these thieves of true life, he would soon see through them.

The whole trouble is, he does not see what he is doing to himself. But he can wake up. He can replace *doing* something with *understanding* something. Walt Whitman writes:

> *You have not known what you are, you have slumbered upon yourself all your life. . . . Whoever you are! claim your own. . . .*

The Essential Factor of Willingness

Keith asked the following questions:

Q. You say that nothing need disturb me, but I can't see how this can be so. If I am insulted or ignored, it hurts.

A. Who gets hurt? The *you* who gets hurt is fictitious, made up of hundreds of wrong ideas about yourself which you take as real. In reality, you are a screen upon which the drama of life is played, but you are not the action itself. Does a movie screen fall apart when a war drama takes place against it? Work to understand this, and hurt goes away forever.

Q. I have a nagging urge to be somebody in life.

A. Why should you be somebody? So that you can join others in the madhouse? Earn your own living, live your own life, and be a decent person. This is being somebody in the right way.

Q. But I don't know what to do.

A. Yes, you know what to do. That is not the problem. You sense the need for giving up stubbornness. Are you willing to pass through the darkness necessary for the destruction of your false self? Wisdom is not required of you; willingness is all you need.

How to Look Above the Human Self

Five men, whose clothes were tattered and who hardly had enough to eat from day to day, heard good news that aroused their hopes for a better life. They were told of a vast treasure to be found on a small and isolated island in the middle of a great lake. Journeying together to the shore, each set out in his own boat. But when a fierce storm arose, *four* of them turned back to the shore. Each gave a shallow reason for quitting:

"I am already rich."
"I believe the report was false."
"It was too lonely in the boat."
"I will try again later on."

None of them dared to speak the truth—that he feared the fierce storm.

But the fifth man, honest and courageous, endured the storm and found the treasure.

Unless we submit to what is above the human self, we cannot shine with what is above. If we insist upon clinging to our dramatizations and evasions, we cannot complain about the suffering they cause.

Will we look at our negativities? That is all we need to do. Yes, right in the midst of the dramatization and the evasion, will we look at them? If so, a fine start has been made, the only kind of start that can end the strife of life.

And we need not fear. The very fear is a product of falseness. As falseness fades, so does fear.

Do not be afraid to live without your fear. Does that sound like a strange thing to say? Yes, we fear to be without fear, for we dread the emptiness which we know will appear when we give it up. Because fear supplies a false sense of aliveness, we cling to it desperately. We feel it is better to be someone who is frightened than to be no one at all, and so we fight to hold onto our very fears.

Fight no longer. Lay down your sword. What you think is out to destroy you is really out to give you eternal life. There is destruction, to be sure, but it is the destruction of a haunted house. To choose quietly what you call self-destruction is actually to choose self-unfoldment. No, you cannot see this as yet, but understanding will come with submission. You will have the light when you accept without resistance what you call darkness.

Yes, it is a frightening experience to plunge fully into your own nothingness, but beyond it is the real, where there is no terror. You see, the Truth both destroys and creates you, but there is a different *you* in each case. The false self is destroyed, while the real self is revealed.

So do not hesitate to enter this mystery, for beyond it is what you have always wanted.

BASIC PRINCIPLES TO THINK ABOUT

1. Esoteric truths can end worries and tensions.
2. The happy ending comes with your own new insights.
3. Inward success is all that counts.
4. You have the capacity to receive the truly valuable.
5. The unattached mind is wonderfully free of worry.
6. Live with your own free and spontaneous nature.
7. Do not pursue life; let it come to you.
8. Perfect living provides fresh energy daily.
9. New personal treasures come through honesty and courage.
10. What you have always wanted, also wants you.

11

How to Place the Whole Universe on Your Side

What does it mean to place the entire universe on your side? It is a mystery to most people, but need not remain one to you. The only thing preventing our alliance with what is truly sensible is our own lack of psychic sight. To place the universe on your side means:

> To be aware of cosmic forces already with you, which need to be awakened, revealed, put to practical use.
> To realize that the placing of these forces on your own side is the same as putting yourself on your own side, for a mind divided against itself cannot stand.
> To admit to a power above our own humanness, which we refuse to do whenever we meet events with resistance, instead of understanding.

How Jerry Placed the Universe on His Side

Jerry M. wanted to open the door to new strength above his own. "You have helped me a lot," he said, "and I want to go on with these things. I sense one of your ideas very personally. You say that we lose our universal strength whenever we depend upon human strength. There is something quite right about this,

130

but I'm too much of a beginner to grasp it. May I have a few clues?"

I replied, "Suppose there is someone in your life from whom you are getting certain things, perhaps friendship or sex or business advantages. This person offends you in some way, so that you feel like telling him or her off. But you hide your true feelings from both yourself and from the other person by remarking, 'Oh, that's all right; I don't mind.' Now, why do you close your eyes to your resentment? Because you fear that expressing how you really feel will lose the supposed benefits. Do you see this?"

Jerry nodded. "Of course. Everyone behaves that way. So what do I do?"

"Understand the whole process. See that you are afraid, which is painful. See that you sacrifice your universal strength, your natural integrity, to supposed benefits. In time you will understand why you need not live this painful way, as most people do."

"That doesn't mean I will tell off everyone who offends me?"

"No, for that is also misunderstanding. The main task is to dare to refuse to cling to human-level benefit for support. Be totally free of them. This opens the door to universal strength, which will surely come."

Jerry's understanding is growing, which means he is placing the entire universe on his side.

HOW TO AROUSE YOURSELF TO COSMIC AWARENESS

Here is a fact of great importance to your understanding of life: Conflict arises when our *personal ideas* contradict what is *universally true.* Now, this is so simple that we might think everyone would want to rush at the chance to drop inaccurate thoughts in favor of what is true. But we have already seen how man is too much in love with his precious little image of being a fountain of wisdom.

It is fantastic how a man refuses to connect the way his day goes with the way his mind works. As a perfect example of how people absently walk into grief, take the matter of personal privacy. No one wants others to poke and pry into his personal affairs. Yet, those with an unhealthy need for certain people will associate with those who love to peep and pry. If this form of annoying trading were understood, it would stop, for no one consciously exposes himself to such prying.

Arouse yourself! See that all your previous efforts to find a simple contentment have not really worked. If they had been right they would have worked. Try to see that no matter what you did or said, you ended up right back where you started. This is not a negative process, nor does it mean the loss of anything of value; to the contrary, you have nothing to lose but nightmares. Many of the letters I receive from readers express delight with their new insight into difficulties which formerly baffled them. That is what you are after—a new way of seeing yourself, after which you live with amazing newness. Start with this practical fact:

Your future is right and bright when you do not try to predict it. Why all this concern over what will happen tomorrow? It is the seeking of security by an insecure self. It hopes to nail down a permanent and undisturbed place for itself. We might as well try to nail a board to a passing stream. Life is change, variety, newness. When clearly seen as such, anxious predicting vanishes.

There is no danger whatsoever in not knowing your psychological future, in not knowing what will happen to you. The only danger is in insistently predicting what it *should* be, for sooner or later your desire will smash itself to pieces against the wall of reality. To prevent this, never protect yourself against the next moment.

Can we let each fresh moment surprise us? Can we cease to resist whatever reality comes our way? Can we let go of the familiar and the known, to enter casually the pureness of the new? If so, we are in happy harmony with the universe.

Let me tell you a story with profound significance. It shows how you can place the entire universe on your side.

Why a Confused Person Smashed His File of Ready-Made Solutions

There was once a young man who feared the confused world he inhabited. In an attempt to protect himself he searched around for defenses and answers and securities. In his ramblings around, he picked up answers from anyone and everyone who offered them. He never questioned their accuracy. To keep these answers handy, he set up a large filing cabinet in his home. The cabinet had thousands of sections labeled *Friendship, Money, Sex, Religion, Marriage, Success* and so on.

After a few years he had files bulging with answers and attitudes with which to meet the challenges of life. For instance, his *Sex* file told him that sex represented excitement, novelty and conquest; his file on *Religion* informed him that to be religious meant to go to church, to pray and to be good.

So he went through his days relying completely upon his ready-made solutions. The system pleased him, for it saved the effort of thinking for himself. Besides, it seemed to provide a proud self-confidence.

But over the years he began to notice several strange things. Even after meeting life with his filing system, a peculiar kind of uneasiness persisted. He also noticed that one answer often seemed to contradict another. For instance, his *Love* file stated that love means to act generously toward others, but another entry from the same file said that love is to place your own integrity first of all.

Also strange was how his filing system caused conflict with other people. He now saw that others also had their own bulging systems opposite to his own, which they angrily defended as being the right systems. The resulting quarrels and hostilities made him gloomy.

Finally, his suffering forced him for the first time to question his filing system. Obviously, it did not provide the peace and protection he wanted, but the very opposite. Also, it shocked him to see how often his files told shameless lies.

Still, he clung to it, for to have on hand such fast answers to everything gave him a sense of individuality, of being not only a commander of his own life but a qualified counselor of others. So he continued to consult his system.

But the pain grew more and more unbearable. He finally saw that he must either abandon the system or continue to suffer. It was a terrible crisis which almost tore him apart. His chief fear was implied when he said, "But if I give it up, how will I meet the crises of daily life? What will become of me?"

One day, unable to endure it any longer, he made up his mind. With mixed courage and terror, he marched to the filing system and broke it up, tossing the pieces into the trash.

The next day he felt lost, abandoned, and his suffering seemed greater than before. But before long a miracle happened all by itself. He felt a great release, a fantastic peace he could hardly believe. But it was there and it was real. There were no more doubts or contradictions, only a pure newness.

Can you, reader, connect this story with yourself?

WHAT YOU NEED NOT DO

Because we live in a mental midnight, we are always doing things that are already being done for us, like a man watering his garden in the rain. Our lives are already being lived for us, but we arrogantly interfere, insisting that we know a better way. And so we nervously build straw houses, while praying that a wind won't come up.

You need not:

Seek love
Defend yourself against anything
Have any self-concern
Be noticed
Be what is called a spiritual person
Anxiously hope for anything
Be considered nice by others
Have security
Plan tomorrow's happiness
Have success on the human level of success

Suppose you stand on a high place to enjoy the beauty of the sparkling sea below. You need do nothing to create that beauty; you need only *be in the same place where it is,* and let nature do the rest. So it is with the inner life. There is nothing we can *do* to gain psychic beauty. It already exists without our effort. We need only be where we belong, that is, in self-union. Then, beauty *is*.

Here is a discussion about deep truths:

Q. For many years I have desperately sought the answers to life. Why have they eluded me?

A. Please do not confuse desperation with earnestness. Desperation prevents earnestness. To be desperate means a refusal to bear the uncertainty of not having answers, which makes you prey to interior illusions and exterior charlatans. The answers come when you are quietly willing to be without them.

Q. Why do you say we must question everything in spiritual matters, instead of having faith and trust?

A. Because much of what is called faith is merely gullibility. Also, deceivers are clever in making stones resemble bread. You may acquire a taste for stones, and in time will be unable to distinguish between stones and bread. And in the final tragedy you will no longer want bread, and will even fight those offering it.

Q. Since hearing you speak I have new thoughts about my self-image. I formerly thought it necessary to have strong images, but you say they are the very barrier to universal strength.

A. The formula is very simple: preserve your image and lose your life; lose your image and preserve your life.

Q. Can this universal wisdom of which you speak make correction of a mistake in the past?

A. You made the mistake because of unawareness, and for no other reason. If you try to correct it while still in psychic sleep, you will merely repeat it in another form. So self-awakening is your only task. Let me emphasize the following fact to you: When you truly and fully learn the lesson from a mistake, you cancel out forever the very mistake itself.

HOW TO FREE YOURSELF FROM MENTAL SLAVERY

David L. called on me one evening after attending one of my Sunday afternoon lectures. He said, "I have studied religion and philosophy long enough to know that self-knowledge is the first sensible step toward true self-transformation. For a long time I proudly thought I knew all about myself, but your books and talks have changed my mind. I suspect that I am, as you put it, a slave to myself. I am at the age where I no longer want to conquer the world, but wish self-conquest. Will you please help me?"

David was using his mind correctly by making this inquiry. He had already made a valuable breakthrough by seeing that *mental slavery consists of refusal to see consciously what we sense unconsciously.* Since this was no longer his attitude, he was receptive to the following ideas we discussed together.

First, we saw that personal freedom must be our *fact,* not our *belief.* If a man believes he is free, but worries over the future, he is not free. If he listens to lectures about freedom, but is disturbed by unpleasant behavior from others, he is unfree. If he talks about a free life, but feels ashamed over past follies, he is in prison.

David remarked, "I now understand why our attention must be given to interior states, not to external conditions."

"Yes, internal freedom must come before external liberty, for, in fact, all freedom is internal. When your mind is liberated from a sense of being insulted or ignored, no one can insult you. A free mind has no self-reference, for there is no false self to be insulted or ignored."

Next, we took up a wrong kind of thinking which bars millions from receiving psychic riches. It is to resist true teachings merely because they are unfamiliar. Isn't *everything* unfamiliar at first? Incidentally, Swiss psychiatrist Carl Jung declared that the esoteric teachings of Buddha—which are largely unfamiliar to Western people—are among the most perfect ever given to mankind.

So I pointed out to David that the sincere seeker need not worry if he fails to grasp right ideas the first time around. If he grasps one out of a hundred he is doing well. Earnest effort is success itself, regardless of results or lack of results.

How David Put the Universe on His Side

David then said, "I really want to get at the heart of things. You are no doubt right when you say that my entire life is an imaginary one. Can you tell me what I am really like?"

"Yes," I replied, "but first I want to explain something that will help you in many ways as you proceed. Most people are terribly afraid of a truthful system that gets too personal with them. They want to keep their distance with pleasant little discussions about reincarnation and psychic powers. The moment you get down to business with personal topics, like self-deception and self-contradiction, they freeze up."

"I'll warm up, instead," he broke in to assure me, "so please proceed."

"I will summarize your actual state in order that you might work intelligently with it. You can work on a fact, but nothing can be done with a fancy. Let me first tell you about some negative states within you. Your attempts to draw good things into your life results in nothing real, and your sensing of this adds despair to the emptiness. You are afraid of what you are doing to yourself, but do not know how to stop. You know that freedom from nagging desires would give you ease, yet fear your nothingness if those desires end. You look forward to rescue from your restlessness by a dinner or an entertainment, but know very well it will return when the party is over."

"Everything you say is accurate," David remarked. "How on earth do you know so much about me?"

"They are true of everyone. But now let me give you some good news. I'll mention four negativities which you are beginning to see through, much as if you were looking into a room through a keyhole. You fearfully suspect that the way you have chosen up to now might have been the hard way after all, which is a small but definite awakening. You wonder whether those whom you have previously depended upon for guidance really know the way out themselves, which means you are starting to think for yourself. You feel your own reluctance to go beyond yourself, but wisely sense its necessity. You despair over ever finding the way out of the haunted house, yet hear the faint whisper that the exit actually exists—which it does."

Nothing but good could come out of a session like that. David received what he wanted and needed—the self-knowledge that puts the universe on his side.

SEVEN STEPS FOR CERTAIN PROGRESS

A group of people once met in a self-improvement session, determined to brave out their criticisms of each other. The turn came for one man, occupying a corner chair, to be criticized. The others pointed out that he was a braggart, generally unreliable, and disliked by most people. The man suddenly stretched, grinned, and remarked, "Sorry, but I fell asleep. I had a great dream about being the dashing leader of a band of romantic adventurers, whom everyone loved and admired. But now, what are your criticisms—if you can find any."

A blunderer has no awareness that he is a blunderer. If he had, he would not be one. His unawareness is his whole problem. Have you ever been in a group of people where one person dominated the conversation with self-centered chatter? That is one type of blundering in the dark. The cure for any kind of blundering is not to suppress it, but to go right ahead and blunder—with all the honesty and impersonal watchfulness of which one is capable.

Do you see why so much emphasis is placed on the need to be an aware man or woman? Awareness is freedom itself. To expect happiness without being an aware person is like expecting the tones of a violin from a trumpet. The right instrument is necessary.

The whole problem is to get an unaware person to see that he *is* unaware, which is not easy. How can he see what he will not see? But there are ways, and one of them is to listen to the lesson of suffering. But even this lesson is resisted, for people love their pains in preference to reality. This is because they have not as yet tasted freedom. An animal accustomed to the confining comforts of his cage will fear the open spaces, and will snap at whoever tries to force him out.

Definite progress can be won by concentrating upon a single aim for a single day. Pour all your energies into doing one thing only, as the following examples indicate:

Sunday: *Observe your changing states of mind.*
Monday: *Do not grumble against anything that happens.*

Tuesday: *Find no pleasure in negative people or events.*
Wednesday: *Snap the spell of mental movies.*
Thursday: *Realize the necessity for psychic awakening.*
Friday: *Have no concern for your status with others.*
Saturday: *Realize that your world is inside you.*

UNFAILING ANSWERS TO VITAL QUESTIONS

A case of milk once fell off a truck, scattering milk and glass all over the street. A small boy paused to look at the mess and asked a bystander, "Why did you break those bottles?" There is no answer to a question like that. Nor are there answers to questions asked in misunderstanding of things as they really are. Instead of looking for answers that do not exist, we must question our own questions until we see their pointlessness.

It is pointless to ask, "I feel that I am quite bad at times, so how can I become a good person?" A clear grasp of universal principles destroys faulty human concepts of "good" and "bad." Is a small child "good" because he knows how to lift a drinking glass to his lips, or is he "bad" because he spills water? No. In the first instance he has learned how to harmonize with the laws of physical movement, in the second instance he has not learned as yet. But there is no personal "good" or "bad" involved.

Here are good esoteric questions asked by my readers:

Q. As a psychologist, I am struck at the almost total lack of communication between people. How do universal principles explain this?

A. There is true communication only when essence speaks to essence. Since most people live from surface personality, instead of essence, the barrier is thick. Only self-free people can understand each other, for they communicate from the single and universal essence, not from a thousand man-made doctrines. The story of the Tower of Babel is an esoteric illustration of human babble.

Q. What does esotericism say about pleasure?

A. True pleasure is the absence of unconscious displeasure. It comes with self-unity, whether we are rich or poor, alone or with others, young or old.

Q. In your book, *The Power of Your Supermind*, you provide some fine ideas about putting labels on things. How can non-labeling aid our quest for universal wisdom?

A. One way is to guard against labeling our feelings in a way that flatters us, but which prevents self-insight. Do not label sentimentality as love, nor stubbornness as determination.

Q. How can I find this new life of which you speak?

A. Detect and extinguish egotism. That is the start and the middle and the end. Detect and extinguish egotism.

HOW TO BANISH TENSION

"I think," Eugene E. told me, "that I can sum up my problem in just a few words. After all my work and hope, I have nothing to show for it."

When I asked him what he wanted to show for it, he admitted confusion about this, also. He added, "I often think of changing my occupation and other things, but have no consistency. One minute I chase off in this direction and the next minute in another. What is going on with me? How can I make right choices?"

If you have ever felt this way, you need only to understand the psychic facts of life.

Life does not present you with hundreds of choices of action and then cruelly withhold judgment as to the right choice. Baffling choices arise from faulty thinking only. With the dawn of understanding, you live choicelessly and cheerfully.

After weighing all the supposed benefits, you choose this future husband or wife over that one. The fault is in thinking that either one can supply the abundant life, which must be found within yourself.

When assaulted by a critical shock, you fall asleep to its lesson by choosing to blame an outside source. The mistake is in trying to escape the shock, instead of letting it awaken you to psychic facts about yourself.

Because your hours are boring and burdensome, you select the stimulation of sex over the stimulation of scoring a financial success. The error is in assuming that any kind of stimulation has true or lasting value.

No one has choices or opinions when he has the facts. Those

who don't know the facts have opinions which they call the facts. Do we have an opinion as to whether the world is round or not? But man's vanity prevents the admission of his lack of facts. To hide his self-deceiving ignorance he resorts to mental gymnastics and loud opinions, from which he suffers.

Take mental pain. Pain exists in the difference between what is fact and what we believe and insist is fact. Pain cannot exist in the fact itself, for pure fact is non-pain. Pain arises when we stretch personal opinion away from cosmic fact. Tension exists in a rubber band only when you stretch it out between two opposing points. If you let the band collapse, tension must also vanish. Likewise, when we release our acquired opinions, the only point left is the fact, in which there is neither tension nor pain.

It is a fact like this which probes and finally lays bare the secrets of the universe—and places those secrets on your side.

VITAL IDEAS FOR REVIEW

1. Universal forces are already within you.
2. Arouse yourself to your vast possibilities.
3. Dare to smash your own fixed filing system!
4. Beauty appears as we return to ourselves.
5. Make inward freedom your personal fact.
6. Self-knowledge provides universal power.
7. Use the seven daily steps supplied in this chapter.
8. True pleasure is the absence of unconscious displeasure.
9. We must abandon opinions in favor of psychic facts.
10. Use these principles to set the universe on your side.

12

How to Stop
Being a Victim of
Cruel or Vindictive People

To cease being hurt and victimized by cruel people, we must understand cruelty itself. We must see why and how it dominates human beings. Reflect carefully upon the following facts, for they are your first necessary steps to freedom.

All human cruelty originates in false ideas about who we are. The vast majority of people live in imaginary ideas about their identities, rather than from facts. But these contradictions are carefully concealed. Here is a man dwelling in a dreamland where he is pleasant and kindly, even spiritual. Now, whatever threatens exposure of this invented self will arouse his cruel and angry attack. He will, of course, cunningly justify it, which means that without the slightest conscience he will tell a lie. He hurts his children or degrades his wife, explaining that it is for their own good, when in fact he does it for fear they may turn out bad and disgrace him. He sees not the slightest contradiction in praying on Sunday and preying on Monday.

As consciousness enables us to drop our pretentious self-pictures, cruelty falls away of itself. It no longer has an unhealthy cause. The soldier whose psychic health no longer needs a self-glorifying medal, will no longer cruelly attack the enemy, for the enemy no longer exists.

As a man becomes his true self, he understands why he was cruel in the past. Consequently, he sees why others are cruel, for they are still in the futile battle from which he happily escaped. In other words, we cease to be victimized by cruel people by uprooting *unconscious* cruelty in ourselves. This means our work is to change the way *we* are, not the way others are. Self-knowledge and self-unity are perfect self-protection.

Have no concern if you do not fully grasp this as yet. Just walk on, remembering that the esoteric way is both *different* and *right*.

HOW TO UNDERSTAND HUMAN NATURE

We must learn to think clearly toward people, including ourselves. Human relations are tragic because people do not really understand each other. There are endless benefits in seeing people, not as they appear to be, but as they actually are.

To do this, imagine a tube containing dozens of marbles of various colors. There is a small window in the tube which permits you to see only one marble at a time. Whenever the tube is shaken, you see a different marble; a red one, a blue one, and so on.

Now, since you understand the inner contents of the tube, it cannot deceive you. If a purple marble appears, you realize it is only one of many, and only temporarily in the window. You do not mistakenly assume that the total nature of the tube is purple. It may be purple one minute, but after the next shake, it may be orange or gray.

This is the exact nature of a man or a woman. He is not a single, consistent, unified person. He appears that way, but the appearance is caused by faulty thinking. Because a person retains the same name, and almost the same physical appearance and mannerisms, we wrongly assume he is as consistent inwardly as outwardly. Not so. He has no single self which controls his behavior. His inner parts are in constant motion, shoving and contradicting each other. As events shake him, he switches from one marble-self to another.

By noticing your experiences with others, and with yourself, you will see how perfectly true this is. One marble-self decides to go on a diet, but is soon replaced by another marble-self that yields to candy. One marble-self wants to be nice to people, but is soon crowded out by a new marble-self with an unpleasant nature.

By grasping this, many mysteries are solved at last. You are no longer exploited. You no longer lose your time or money or happiness to deceitful people. You realize that lofty statements are no evidence of lofty natures; you sense that the man who smiles may simply be a smiling scoundrel.

The first place to see this lack of inner unity is in ourselves. It is achieved through persistent practice in the art of Silent Seeing. Awareness of changeability and contradiction within ourselves has power for self-unity, placing us in command of our own health and happiness.

WHY YOUR TRUE NATURE CANNOT BE HURT

Kathryn D., an office worker, came to tell me about a certain resentment she had toward those with whom she worked. It started when her marriage began to break up. To her amazement and resentment, she found herself facing a firing squad of prying questions. She admitted to inviting a certain amount of it, for she had a need to talk with someone. But she was shocked to detect the pleasure with which others heard her unhappy story. There was an avalanche of advice, most of it stupid, and obviously from bitter women. And eventually, gossip about Kathryn drifted back to her.

"I think," Kathryn said, "that human beings, beneath their thin veils of decency, are nothing more than vicious animals who will use anything for their own pleasure. Why, those people were having the time of their lives with my grief, disguising it as friendship. Mr. Howard, I am not bitter about this; I simply see the fact. It is a shock, but a healthy one. I would never have believed that this is the way people really are, unless I had read your books."

How Kathryn Broke Out of Her Resentments

Kathryn was one of those with a persistent wish to break out. This was not the first crisis in her life; previous ones had urged her toward inner exploration. She was therefore ready to use this crisis for psychic advancement, which meant the gradual lessening of such griefs. The following ideas helped Kathryn, as they can also help you.

If you were truly a mind reader, you would soon lose all your idealistic notions about people. For one thing, you would see that most of what passes for generosity is either an attempt to relieve guilt or to make a favorable impression. *"In truth, I am glad to get away from these actors . . . who are as ungrateful for my benefits as they are false in their pretensions of piety."* (Erasmus)

Usually, when we are with others, we notice only their surface selves, such as facial features and physical mannerisms. But for beneficial insight into human nature, try something entirely different. When you meet another, try to see his *psychological self.* Be aware of his motives for doing what he does. Notice his nervousness; watch how his conversations center around himself.

You see, insight into others is an aid for returning to our true nature, which cannot be harmed by human folly. As Henri Frederic Amiel explains, *"My true being, the essence of my nature, myself, remains inviolate and inaccessible to the world's attacks."*

How Self-Freedom Protects You Against the Hurts of Life

Here are some questions and answers which came up during a frank discussion with Mr. and Mrs. Kenneth C., who were studying with me:

Q. Mr. Howard, please explain how self-freedom protects us from the hurts of life.

A. There can be attacks *toward* you but not *against* you. Attacks from others have no target to hit, for the free man is psychologically invisible. How can a tossed brick hurt the air? Attacks can hit and hurt only the hardened ego-self. If this disappears, who is there to hurt?

Q. You say that unless esoteric principles are first understood, it is useless to engage in what society calls acts of goodness, such as giving to charity. I don't understand.

A. If we really want to help a sick society we must first stop our own unconscious participation in its sickness. A self-deceived man has nothing of true value to give, which is the state of almost everyone. I knew a woman who one day showed great public sympathy for a cat which was stuck in a tree-top. That same sympathetic woman destroyed her children's lives by her private example of hatred and bitterness.

Q. Sometimes I angrily blow up at people, which makes me ashamed. What is the matter with me? You can speak bluntly.

A. Why are you ashamed of your explosions, not of their smoldering causes? I will tell you. You are ashamed because the explosions expose your pretense of *not* having that resentful volcano within. You have had it all your life. Instead of shame, why not study your explosions from the esoteric viewpoint? Why continue to suffer?

Q. If you have done one thing, you have made me horribly aware of the greedy grab of human beings for power and authority. Everyone wants to command someone else. And until we studied with you, we would never have believed it was also in us, at least to some degree. How does esotericism explain the human craving for power over others?

A. Human puppets have a neurotic need to create other human puppets, so as to provide the illusion of being the masterful puppeteers. But their inevitable failure condemns them to dangle in their own darkness.

Q. How can I change my associations, so that I no longer get involved with the wrong people?

A. As sincere self-work raises your level of consciousness, your associations change automatically, just as rising in an airplane provides purer air.

THE POWER OF ALERTNESS

People confess, "I just don't know how to behave when with other people, especially strangers. I usually conceal my nervousness behind empty chatter, as does everyone else. I know there's something wrong with this, but that's how I am."

That's how most people are. All because they are trying to protect something—heaven knows what. Most public behavior is a mechanical performance. Watch it for yourself. You know exactly what a man will say because he always says it. He performs what might be called substitute behavior. Unable to flow freely and spontaneously from his natural essence, he substitutes his old and monotonous ways.

Look what happens on the social level, when society faces a tough problem. What do the leaders do? They form committees, and have investigations and hearings. Why? Because no one really has the slightest notion of what to do. They hope that the shared confusion will somehow conceal individual ignorance.

Any earnest person can break away from social chaos and nervousness. He can do so by calling upon a particular esoteric force, which is introduced as follows.

My front yard is a passing parade of chipmunks, ravens, roadrunners and other small creatures. The frisky chipmunk is a good example of this special esoteric force. Wherever he dashes, whatever he does, the chipmunk's chief characteristic is *alertness*. His bright eyes swiftly spot the bread set out for him. He carries it off to his high rock, where he perches and munches, while in alert observation of his surroundings. Alertness pays the chipmunk. It will pay us, too.

How to Build Alertness

Mental alertness is blunted by daydreams and especially by anxious emotions. If a woman is concerned with what others think of her, she cannot be aware that it makes no difference at all what others think of her. So our first step is to be alert to our own unalertness.

Whenever you are with others, alertly use your opportunities for a deeper understanding of human nature. Remember, the more uncomfortable the situation, the more it will reward you— if you work.

Suppose you give something to someone, not because you really wanted to give it, but because you felt it was expected of you. If you can attentively watch this feeling as it arises, you have gained valuable self-acquaintance. Suppose you sense that a person who claims to like you is quite capable of turning against you at the slightest excuse. By going beyond the sensing, to be clearly aware of it, you have broken a link in a psychic chain around yourself.

Let every crisis in your human relations serve as a signal for your alertness, for example:

> An alert pause, instead of an impulsive move
> An alert observation, in place of a judgment
> An alert understanding, rather than a criticism
> An alert inquiry, in place of a conclusion
> An alert reflection, instead of an opinion
> An alert listening, in place of a remark
> An alert learning, rather than an advising
> An alert quietness, instead of an aggressiveness

THE FALLACY OF SATISFYING YOUR EGO

The trading of ego-gratification is the basis of most human relations, which uninformed humans call love and unity. A person who you think is the nicest, kindest, most loyal person on earth will abandon you instantly when: (1) You hurt his ego. (2) Cease to feed his ego. (3) Cease to serve his ego as much as someone else.

So esotericism calls upon what is truly heroic in you, by asking the question: *Do you want to go through life painfully and nervously trading worthless trinkets with others, or do you want eternal riches? If you try to compromise, you will have your friends, but you will lose the more abundant life. Stand alone. Be true. Then, the people in your life will be the right ones for you.*

Do not let others rule your life. Never mind what they think of you. Do not assume that it is essential for you to keep their goodwill. To do so is to exchange what is true in you for the worthless beads of their good opinion of you. You must stop all this. It is wearing you down and gaining you nothing, for they have nothing to give you.

What Really Matters in Liberating Yourself

I have on my desk a letter from Carl C., who has finally realized these liberating truths. He writes, "I finally understand, *really* understand, that it matters not at all what others think of me. In the first place, the majority of human beings do not think truly, with real love; they merely react mechanically, according to acquired mental habits. Their thinking is dominated by negative self-seeking. I am not being self-righteous; I know too well the dark corners in myself requiring psychic sunshine."

Carl's observations continue, "The study of esotericism has made one thing unmistakably clear. The only thing that matters is what *I* think. No one else can direct my destiny. So my aim in life is to think purely, unhampered by false needs for attention and for what society calls respect."

Carl is right. He has ventured beyond his usual self, coming up with a testimony both original and refreshing.

HOW TRUE PLEASURE IS DEVELOPED

Carl's insight into the wrongness of human ways is supported by those who saw deeply into human nature as it actually is. The Dutch teacher, Erasmus, pointed out, *"The larger part of mankind . . . is subject to folly."* Friedrich Nietzsche adds, *"When they give themselves out as wise, then do their petty sayings and truths chill me. . . ."*

A certain challenge may arise upon reaching the level of insight gained by Carl. You may feel that the seeing of people as they really are, may rob you of the pleasures of their company. If so, esoteric principles race to the rescue. You see, genuine pleasure is that which springs from your own private essence, not from public attractions. True pleasure has no dependency upon the presence or favors of others. Self-pleasure is *self-pleasure.*

It does not depend upon the excitement of a particular individual, nor upon crowds. Any friend capable of giving you mere excitement is no friend of yours. Excitement is a false god which lures you away from your essence, where true pleasure abides. You see, anything exterior to you with the seeming power for pleasure, also has power to plunge you into gloom.

Of course, the esoteric way includes friends and social enjoyments, but their nature is different. Your relations with others are on true terms, with you in calm command. You do not give integrity in exchange for thrills, for you know better.

Like Carl, we must see the difference between true and false pleasure; this insight carries us toward the true. The mystical Henry Suso supplies a magnificent declaration: *"What greater pleasure is there than to find myself the one thing that I ought to be, and the whole thing that I ought to be?"*

You do not plan a vacation by using a map printed thirty years ago. To do so would spoil your fun. You need what is right for you *today*. Most people wander the world of human relations with maps printed on their minds decades ago, making everything wrong. You can go right with the new ideas you have just read.

TWENTY VALUABLE SECRETS ABOUT HUMAN NATURE

1. The more a person demands love and consideration from others, the less he is able to give them to others.

2. You truly understand another when you see him free from your personal feeling toward him.

3. Beware of those who promote their own egotism by cunning appeals to the egotism in others.

4. "If you want to discover your real opinion of anyone, observe the impression made upon you by the first sight of a letter from him." (Arthur Schopenhauer)

5. Never let another person's resentment or impatience intimidate you.

6. The worst motive anyone could ever have for doing something is to attract the notice of others.

7. The facts about a man are only as real as he is.

8. If we really want to be original, we must stop being confused, for to be confused is the most commonplace thing on earth.

9. Don't get tired of your boss; get tired of your own irritation toward the boss.

10. Human beings are experts at faking anything, and are most expert at faking pleasantness.

11. "But there is much lying among small people." (Friedrich Nietzsche)

12. Do not let the unhappy lives of other people interfere with your happiness.

13. If you searchingly ask, "Who is it out there who makes me run so hard?" you will not find anyone who does so.

14. The best way to become a victim of sick society is to wish to appear respectable in its eyes.

15. Be friendly to everyone, but for or against no one.

16. Never judge a person's friendliness toward you while he still wants something from you.

17. Sick people seek out other sick people, and when they meet they hurt each other.

18. Politicians are not the representatives of the awakened man.

19. An early sign of self-awakening is when you see both yourself and others in a new light.

20. The only power on earth capable of freeing us of painful experiences with others is esoteric self-knowledge.

HOW SELF-INSIGHT PROVIDES SELF-HARMONY

There is a sure way to understand other people, which frees us of foolish involvements and allows general harmony. It is really quite simple, but will we *do* it? We really understand others only if we really understand ourselves. Our delusions concerning others are of the same degree as our delusions about ourselves.

Esoterically, the worse we get, the better we get. The average person lives from self-flattering images of being so nice and wise and strong, but self-flattering images are all they are. That is what keeps him in hot water with himself and with others. When we don't resist our own evil by setting up opposite and phony self-pictures of being good, the evil disappears.

What a supreme moment when we accept ourselves as we are at the present moment—with all our anger and pride· and stupidity—and yet hear the faint whisper that it need not remain that way!

How Carol Was Healed of Sniping at Others

Carol A. heard that whisper. She had endured a certain inner disturbance for many years before gaining enough courage to speak about it. But she had worked upon herself long enough to see the problem as residing within herself.

She said, "I am a sniper. I snipe at people, sometimes out loud and sometimes in my mind. I am critical, often unkind. One part of me wants to hurt others, while another part senses its wrongness. Can you explain me to myself?"

Carol was not alone in her problem; she was merely more honest than most people. What is the answer to this form of compulsive self-destruction?

Why We Want to Hurt Others

We hurt others, either openly or cunningly, as a reaction to our own inner hurt. Pain produces pressure. Henri Frederic Amiel writes: *"We are never more discontented with others than when we are discontented with ourselves. The consciousness of wrongdoing makes us irritable, and our heart in its cunning, quarrels with what is outside it, in order that it may deafen the clamour within."*

It is important to understand the cosmic law that cruelty toward another is also cruelty toward ourselves. The same torch with which we ignite our neighbor's house will also ignite our own. If we can give up the false pleasure gained from burning down our neighbor's home, we automatically cease to destroy our own. This takes self-insight which itself requires much sincere self-work. But why not work at it, since our own homes are in danger?

As insight heals our personal ache, there is no longer public aggressiveness. This is true freedom, having no cunning or repression. So here is something anyone can understand about himself. It makes the individual instrument harmonious, in tune with itself, whether the rest of the orchestra is in tune or not.

UNERRING PATHS TO OMNIPOTENT LOVE

What does the mystic, or psychic influence say about love? A Sufi mystic named Jal Rumi writes, *"Love is the remedy of our pride and self-conceit, the physician of all our infirmities."*

But we have work to do, for to achieve true love we must first detect and banish what most human beings *label* as love.

Self-centered ambition has no love, for everything outside it must be sacrificed to its compulsive needs, though these needs will parade around as compassion. What the duck hunter calls good is bad for the duck.

There is no such thing as mass love or organized compassion. This virtue is always the individual expression of those few who have truly broken through themselves, to come out on the other side, where cosmic love exists. What foolish society calls an organized effort toward human love and brotherhood is nothing more than the herd-instinct of its members for self-promotion and self-protection.

True love comes as we drop words and live from essence, as the following story illustrates.

A pair of boys, living near each other in the countryside, were good friends. They had great fun in their companionship, roaming the woods and fields. As they grew older, they visited the big city, where they first heard of human brotherhood and of charitable attitudes. Wherever they went, they heard sermons and read books on the subject of being good to others.

Because it sounded reasonable, they tried to practice what they heard preached. But, strangely, the more they made an effort to like each other, the more strained their relationship became. And for the first time, they quarreled.

Sensing that something was wrong, they forgot the sermons and together went back to the countryside. Once more they enjoyed the adventure of the woods and fields.

There is only one basic love, which is love for the Truth itself. When the Truth is our foundation, its expressions will be authentic and tender, including love for spouse and children and friend.

CHAPTER HIGHLIGHTS FOR SELF-COMMAND IN HUMAN RELATIONS

1. We must understand the nature of human cruelty.
2. Study human nature at every opportunity.

3. Whoever lives from his true nature cannot be hurt.
4. Place acts of cosmic perception before acts of goodness.
5. Your own right thinking is all that matters.
6. Self-knowledge supplies authentic self-command.
7. Use human relations as exercises in self-insight.
8. Place self-harmony first, and all else follows.
9. To live from our essence is to live in love.
10. Love the Truth above all.

13

Transcendental Answers to the Mysteries of Life

Many wondrous experiences will occur as you progress toward esoteric understanding. We will explore some of them in this chapter.

How to Solve the Mystery of Authentic Self-Transformation

Imagine a thousand blocks of wood of all shapes and sizes. They are about to pass through a machine which can fashion them into human figures. The first step is to cut away the rough bark. Next, any weaknesses in the wood are cut off. The third step consists in shaping the head and shoulders, and so on. The blocks of wood which resist a particular stage, cannot go on to the next. For instance, if a hard part of a block refuses to be cut away, the entire block is then unfit. But those pieces offering no resistance to the transforming process, come out as human figures. That is the process of self-change we have been discussing throughout these pages.

How to Penetrate the Mystery of Invisible Guidance

In your early years of self-work, you may need aid from those who have achieved the heights for themselves. But as you ascend personally, the former aids and encouragements gradually disappear. There will be no panic when this happens; to the contrary, there is confident single-mindedness. The need for encouragement exists only while its opposite, discouragement, still exists within us. When resting upon the heights, there is no exterior aid or guidance, for you no longer need them. When you are on top of the mountain, do you still need the trail?

You Will Solve the Mystery of How to End Anxiety

Picture yourself standing on the shores of a lake, watching your reflection in the restless waters. If you take the reflection as being *you,* anxiety arises, for the waters constantly change and distort the image. You feel insecure, with neither identity nor stability. But when you see the image *as* an image, when you no longer identify yourself with the changing reflections, trouble ceases forever.

EXCITING EXPERIENCES YOU MAY EXPECT

Some experiences will be strange indeed. Some day, when you have broken through a bit, you may find yourself part of a congregation where you suspect that falsehood is offered as truth. The speaker may tell a funny story. Others may laugh, but you must not laugh. It is not funny.

And some experiences will be magnificent. If you try to make the world come to you, it will not come; but if you cease trying, the world will come, but it will be a world entirely different from the one you tried to attract.

Some adventures will reveal the workings of psychic laws. On several occasions, while conducting some business at a certain office, I noticed the despair of the woman in charge. Suppressed anguish seeped out into her eyes and movements. I wanted to tell her, "It need not be that way at all." I could not do so, for it would have been against a definite psychic law. That law states that nothing can be given to a sufferer unless he *asks of himself,* and *with at least a trace of sincerity.* In her present state, my words would have wrongly fallen on her need for comfort, rather than rightly on her wish for understanding. The yearning for comfort prevents understanding. Jesus explained this law by saying that pearls must not be cast before swine, that is, before those who are unready.

Make yourself ready, for in your receptive state you will see that:

> The whole world, except for the few awakened individuals, lives from imaginations, which are taken as realities.
> The Truth is always introducing itself to us. We fail to see it, because we are looking the other way.
> Others can present a truth to you, but no one can confirm it to you but yourself.
> Almost all of what is called human enthusiasm is merely a frantic distraction from a sense of inner emptiness.
> Your perfect teacher is named Daily Experience.
> You need not desperately try to be good, but work to be real, which alone is good.
> If you are really in charge of yourself, no one else can possibly take charge of you.
> The greatest doctor on earth is honesty, for where there is pure honesty, there can be no pain.
> You must be willing to be wrong in the world's eyes, if you are ever to be right in your own.
> Whatever is done from your own understanding will be exactly right.

HOW A SALESMAN ACQUIRED VALUABLE SELF-KNOWLEDGE

Roger C. was obviously a man with a troubled mind. He started by saying how difficult it had been for him to come and see me. He apologized for cancelling a previous appointment, explaining that he had been so overwhelmed by a sense of futility toward life that it seemed useless even to try any longer.

"If this is all there is to life," he said, "I wonder whether it's worth the effort to go on. I used to have what I called willpower, but even that has gone. When I heard about you, I thought there might be a last hope."

I gave Roger a wondrous fact which is given at the beginning

of this book. I told him that esotericism is definitely not for people who are good or strong or successful. It can only help a failure
who willingly accepts the knowledge of failure.

Roger smiled at that statement, saying, "If failure is a requirement, I'm ready."

Roger's work as a salesman brought him into daily contact
with dozens of people. I pointed out the value of using these
contacts for self-knowledge. He did so, which gave his life new
meaning. One of our later discussions went like this:

> **Q.** I see quite clearly the way in which we bring distress
> upon ourselves. How can I help relieve the punishment a
> friend has brought upon himself?
>
> **A.** You must not try to relieve the psychological punish-
> ment one brings upon himself. It cannot be done. With your
> own self-awakening, you will act from natural essence toward
> this person, which is the only true help.
>
> **Q.** You have certainly hit one thing exactly on target. The
> more I detect my own phoniness, the more I see it in others.
> It seems that everyone is waiting to pounce on whoever passes
> by.
>
> **A.** All unawakened people are pouncers. The ego-self sits
> around and cunningly watches for its own advantage in any
> situation, appearing pleasant and cooperative when hoping
> for benefits, but turning sour and critical when denied.
>
> **Q.** I am kept in tension by wondering about another's atti-
> tude toward me. How can I relax?
>
> **A.** Through self-knowing. You will then see that another's
> attitude toward you, whether gentle or harsh, is entirely be-
> side the point. The essential self is unaffected by such things.

HOW TO DISSOLVE SHOCK AND DISAPPOINTMENT

There is a fascinating experiment by which you can understand life-events.

Watch what happens after experiencing a disappointing result.
As a consequence, it leads you to another result which you label
as satisfying. Next, follow that satisfying outcome and it will
sooner or later lead you to another disappointment. In other

words, watch how your feelings constantly swing back and forth between pleasure and disappointment.

For example, a man fails to get a promotion, causing disappointment. Later, he feels good when his promoted rival is required to move to a less pleasant city. Still later, he suffers an ache when hearing of the other man's higher salary. And so he swings from gloom to elation, elation to gloom. He finds this to be true of all of life's events.

What is the point? This is no way to live. It is not living at all. It is a monotonous and nervous swinging between gloom and false elation. But by living from the central self, there is liberation from both of these opposites.

All shocks and disappointments connect in some way to a false sense of self. This is why an intense exploration of the nature of the self is essential to you. The natural sunlight of the mind breaks through as we dispel the clouds of misunderstanding.

So, do not think that the beginning of some exterior event will also be the beginning of new happiness. True happiness has neither beginning nor end; it is just here, always here, ready for your realization.

The Correct Response to External Events

What is the correct response to external events? The only healthy response is passive awareness of them. This requires explanation, for the idea of quiet observation disturbs people. They object, "But how can passive awareness solve anything? We must take action!"

Yes, and that is exactly why the entire world is in chaos. We act without basic intelligence. Passive awareness moves the artificial self away from an event, enabling cosmic intelligence to act through us. This intelligence is without the rash egotism of the invented self. When we are quietly aware of something, we see it clearly, without the disturbing influence of selfish motives.

Sooner or later, we must understand that there is nothing to *get* from external events, only something to *see*. From the esoteric viewpoint, seeing *is* getting.

There is no need whatsoever to be disappointed at anything that happens to you. Why? Because there is absolutely no denial of anything we really need. Therefore, we must examine our thinking that we need a thing, rather than objecting to its denial.

HOW TO LET ACCUSATIONS WORK TO YOUR BENEFIT

If we really mean business about inner transformation, the denial of what we want is one of the finest experiences we can have. The denial sets up conflict, which points out our separation from peaceful reality. But if we fail to observe our grief arising from denial, we will fail to see its cause. If I fail to understand the cause of my pain at someone's attacking my pet belief, I will not realize the flimsy and worthless character of my belief. I must see the psychic causes of all my pains, after which it becomes my pleasure to abandon them.

Not to know what will happen to you is no cause of anxiety. It is not worth the slightest thought on your part. You are being cared for in a way which you cannot see as yet. Once you see, you will take no thought for tomorrow. Your task is not to know the events of tomorrow, but to know the true self of today.

So do not hesitate to work on yourself. Yes, you hesitate toward the very liberty for which you yearn. But it is only because you are unaware of the true nature of freedom. It is not out to take anything of value from you; it seeks only to remove the shocking and the disappointing. The aim is to give you back to yourself.

All your friends are miserable in some way. Admitted or not, that is their actual condition. If you don't want to live in misery, you must start to react differently to life. I will show you a superb way to start.

Have you ever noticed how terribly a man fears to be blamed and accused? Sternly ask someone, "Did you do that?" and he tenses up defensively. Watch it in yourself. Now, you must start reacting to all forms of blame in an entirely new way. *You must not defend yourself,* or more accurately, *you must not defend what you call yourself,* for you are not who you think you are.

So, whenever accused, do not resist the accusation, but let it fall upon a non-defensive mind. Whether or not you were actually at fault is entirely beside the point; your only task is not to defend your mental position—but let the accusation destroy something faulty in you. There is something faulty and harmful or else the accusation would not have caused grief in the first place.

This may seem like a small thing, but over the years I have found it amazingly effective for breaking into the sunlight.

SECRETS FOR INSTANT HELP FOR YOURSELF

1. The world does not need your money or charitable activities or your generosity with your human-level talents. It needs your spiritual maturity, for only that has real power to transform anything for the better.

2. *If a man truly wishes more psychic strength, those who can aid him will be seen as friends. But if he secretly prefers his darkness, helpers will be seen as enemies. It all depends upon what a man really prefers.*

3. No truth is *our* truth in the sense that we originate or maintain it. It is ours in a much grander sense; we *are* the very truth itself in our essential natures. When realized, it destroys egotism and self-righteousness, making us right at last.

4. *When we finally see that we are all in the same boat, we never think harshly of anyone. The absence of unconscious harshness is authentic love.*

5. The question might arise, "If esotericism can change the world, why hasn't it done so?" The answer is, "Where did you ever get the notion that the masses of mankind want esotericism? Who wants to be told he has been living in stupid vanity all his life?"

6. *Whatever a man worships has power to injure him. But the injury is not caused by some outside god, for there is none. Injury comes from the false god within, which is projected outwardly by his fears and desires. A man is injured only by his own illusions, which he worships as gods.*

7. You should live as if there were not a single man-made system which can punish your psychic self, nor a single man-made

system which can reward it, for that is the truth. Free yourself of the notions of social punishment and reward, and you will know what it means to be a real man.

8. *A lazy man gets nowhere because he snuggles down in what he calls his "faith" or "philosophy of life." The sincere man accepts nothing which he cannot feel is right for him; he verifies everything through individual thinking.*

9. Whenever we hear an esoteric truth, we can either absorb it or we can imitate it. If we imitate, we become self-righteous preachers; if we absorb, we become genuine people.

10. *If we have false values we get false rewards, but will not see them as such. If we have right values, we get right rewards and consciously enjoy them as such.*

HOW YOU CAN ATTUNE TO HEAR COSMIC TRUTH

Parents of teenagers know how it feels to see a son or daughter stubbornly pursuing a reckless course leading to sure tragedy. The parents know that the child is psychologically deaf; he cannot hear their warnings. In this manner does a teacher of esotericism watch the violence and stupidity of mankind, knowing that it cannot hear the truth. When a man in psychic slumber is told an esoteric truth, *he does not hear.* His hardened mind is unable to translate words into cosmic meaning. Therefore, he dismisses it as valueless, or as something which he already knows.

It will be valuable for us to observe the process of *esoteric hearing.* First of all, we hear an esoteric fact. If we welcome it, a small bell rings inside. Even though it disturbs our previous opinions, we sense its rightness. For instance, we faintly realize the folly of pretending to know something which we really don't know.

But this fact now encounters hundreds of obstacles thrown up by the ego-self which senses a threat to its false hold. It immediately begins a counterattack, creating conflict within the individual. The false parts within the person, the parts which don't want the truth, express themselves in various negativities, such as aggressiveness, lying, sarcasm, and sometimes in physical violence.

However, even with this, the sincere seeker is well on his way. He can be conscious of this process; he can observe how his false parts oppose what his true parts want. His very awareness of what is taking place inside him places him in command. More and more he is able to say *no* to the darkness and say *yes* to the light. Mr. and Mrs. Wesley R. sought the light with these questions:

Q. We once heard that deeper truths can be taught in silence between teacher and pupil. Is that true?

A. Yes. Silence says something quite profound when teacher and pupil communicate intuitively. Without saying a word, both *know*.

Q. We agree that human beings are terrible hypocrites, but doesn't the seeing of this make us upset and critical?

A. If there is distress or criticism in our seeing the deceit of humanity, we do not truly understand it, but are still part of it.

Q. You say we must be earnest about the inner life. What is your definition of earnestness?

A. Earnestness means to study a single idea for ten years, if necessary, until you understand it.

Q. Please explain what you mean by unconscious slavery?

A. Take someone who worries over money matters, perhaps a businessman who fears the failure of a certain project. Unless he observes the movement of his mind, he cannot detect his unconscious slavery to worry. Incidentally, do you really think that the human world of finances is higher than cosmic law? That is exactly what you think if you worry over money in any way. You can break the chains of all financial worries.

WHEN YOU DON'T KNOW WHAT TO DO ABOUT A PROBLEM

The Taoist sages said, *"Perfect happiness is the absence of happiness."* Now, this is a very deep principle, with hidden wealth. It means that whoever has lots of ideas about what it means to be happy is *unhappy.* For instance, a man's idea of happiness is to travel or to follow sports or to build his career. A woman's idea of gladness is to be married, have a family. But what happens to their happiness if reality denies these ideas or takes them away? Do you see the point? Mere ideas, mere desires, are subject to denial and change by external happenings.

But what if a man has no ideas whatsoever as to what will make him happy? Do you see what this means? It means that nothing on earth can take away his gladness. Having nothing, he has nothing to lose. There can be no clash between his ideas about life and what life actually presents to him. Such a man is unified, complete, free.

Let me express the same thought in a slightly different way: If you had no ideas whatsoever as to what you *should* do with yourself today, today would be lived freely, spontaneously, happily.

Upon meeting these ideas, one of my readers wrote me:

> *One of your points fascinates me. You say that not to know what to do about something includes the very answer itself. I suspect an esoteric fact of great value here, but do not see it clearly. Will you please explain?*

I replied:

> *Do you have a problem when you don't know what to do about something? Of course not. When you are totally blocked in every direction, when there is no way out, when the mind has exhausted its efforts, how can you have a problem? There is only the plain fact that there is no exit whatsoever. So what is there to fight? The problem arises only when you believe there are several ways out, but do not know which one to take. You are in conflict because you desire the supposed benefits of one choice, but fear losing the supposed benefits of another choice. All this means you are wrongly trying to perpetuate a false sense of self through the supposed benefits.*
>
> *Perhaps an example will help. When you absolutely do not know what to do when someone hurts your feelings, you will then do nothing at all, but this* NOTHING *is the right response. But if you think you know what to do—perhaps get angry or depressed—these choices are not proper responses at all, but mechanical and self-harming reactions.*
>
> *Dare to give up all choice in psychological matters. It will not be easy at first, for your choices are giving you a false sense of individuality, which you fear to abandon. But experi-*

ment with it, try to understand what it all means. Your understanding sets you free of the frustrations involved in choice. You will walk down a single path, with no crossroads.

HOW TO COPE WITH COMPULSIVE THOUGHTS

I recall Betty J. who told me, "I know there are many wondrous discoveries ahead, for I have had tiny glimpses. You have made it clear that to *be* is what counts, not to *do*. I used to try to convert others to my beliefs—the very beliefs which made me miserable! Also, you once told me that if I really loved my children I would straighten out my own life to serve as an example of serenity. I'm afraid I didn't like the counsel at the time, but of course you are right."

I asked her, "What are you working on just now?"

"I am trying," she replied, "to grasp what you say about compulsive thinking. Before you pointed it out I was totally unaware of the obsessive nature of my thoughts; I *had* to think. What causes these mental riots?"

"It is quite possible to let them go, but a man refuses to do so because he fears he would be alone and empty without them. They supply a False Feeling of Life. It is like a man who won't leave a dangerous street riot because he fears returning to his lonely apartment. A man will do almost anything except come face to face with his silent mind, which is his deliverance."

"I see. I must dare to drop compulsive thoughts."

"Do so, remembering that it does not lead to a *vacant* mind, but to a *new* mind."

"What relief that would be."

"That is the perfect description—*relief*."

"Well, you have given me something else to think about. You have no idea, Mr. Howard, how much I appreciate all you have done for me. I shudder to think how I might have walked right by all this, not sensing its incredible richness. Please be patient with me; there is so much I need to know."

Betty has one bright gem of understanding: Our desire must not be to act or talk or choose or believe or dream—but to *know*.

When understanding comes, you are a law unto yourself, which is a wondrous state. You will not break this law, either personally or socially, for it is your very own nature, and you will not go against yourself. It is the same as a peach tree which remains true to its own nature by producing peaches, not sour apples.

And that is truly a wondrous secret.

CHAPTER REVIEW OF THE ANSWERS TO LIFE'S MYSTERIES

1. Esotericism explains the great mysteries of life.
2. Your competent teacher is named Daily Experience.
3. Self-knowledge provides authentic self-relaxation.
4. Respond to external events the esoteric way.
5. Your true nature is above shock and disappointment.
6. Take blame and accusation with a non-defensive mind.
7. Right values bring right rewards.
8. Learn to listen to esoteric whisperings.
9. Happiness is ours when we truly understand its nature.
10. Wondrous secrets presently exist within your own nature.

14

How You Can Turn into an Entirely New Person

Do not be heavily solemn about all this depth of thought. Be earnest and thoughtful, but do not study with a heavy mind. There is nothing to be heavy about, in fact, every line you read in this book is really light-hearted good news.

Good news? No doubt you will agree it is good news that:

Cosmic or Psychic insight provides the effortless life.
Unhappiness exists as a fact, but not as a necessity.
The way out can be found by you.
The Third Way of Thinking is a miraculous power.
You can begin a new life by seeing things in esoteric light.

HOW LOSS CAN MEAN GAIN

A man discovered a new region in which to live. A few days after settling himself, a violent storm swept over the land. He trembled with fear over what he believed to be his great loss. However, to his surprise, the storm swept away only the unrooted and useless. He was grateful for the storm which had revealed and removed the useless.

That is how psychic storms can work for our benefit. To observe conflicts and contradictions within ourselves is no cause for dismay. They are present only because there are things you do not as yet understand. This lack of knowledge is no problem. All you need to do is achieve understanding. Then, the psychic storm ceases.

One woman told me that while she did not as yet grasp the esoteric principle of self-observation, she sensed its importance. That is how necessary knowledge comes to us: by a faint whispering, which eventually turns into clear hearing.

Let me ask a question of those who have entered the esoteric way, even a short distance: Do you hear that faint whispering that here at last is something *real?*

HOW TRUE RICHES COME TO YOU

Growth toward true values cannot occur unless there is *first* the loss of false values. Loss of the false makes room for the true. So your first aim is to detect what is wrong, not to gain what is right. The true comes automatically, just as the freshness of spring follows the fading of winter.

How can we start losing the false? By honestly recognizing it as such. We must simply see how falseness has tricked and punished us all these years. When I actually see what envy and anger are doing to me, I have no more taste for them. Psychic success comes through a steadfast contemplation of whatever is factual about oneself.

Whatever is real within you cannot be stolen by fickle fortune. Whatever can be lost is not worth keeping. So why complain about losing anything? It is a man's fear that complains, "You are taking something of value from me!" Reality replies, "Let it go completely, and you will no longer see it as valuable."

The following ideas were discussed with Arnold M.:

> Q. I sense the need for personal effort, which clears up a former puzzle. I used to wonder why you emphasized the need for independent search.
>
> A. Yes, by working with society, we get society's delusions. Only independent search reveals the inner kingdom. Otherwise, we have the pathetic and dangerous situation of teachers who don't really know, teaching those who don't really want to know.

Q. I am beginning to see the useless chattering of my mind. I know how it drains my energy, but can't seem to stop.

A. Do you know the real dread of a man upon arising in the morning? It is the realization that here is another day in which he must *think.* A bird wanders restlessly when it cannot find its own nest. By ceasing to seek deliverance outside the self, the split mind is healed, bringing rest.

Q. It is wonderful to hear you explain how pain can be used to end pain. How can I end the pain of discouragement?

A. By seeing egotism as the cause of discouragement. Discouragement means you are face to face with the fact that you are not a dictator who can demand that results match your desires. See this, submit your ego to destruction by reality, and discouragement becomes impossible. Incidentally, you must not secretly love discouragement, for this provides a harmful False Feeling of Life.

COSMIC WISDOM IS WITHIN YOUR MIND

Whenever a spiritual system is offered to you, try to see everything you can about it. Try to see whether you accept it as relief from anxiety, or reject it because it contradicts your usual beliefs. Both reactions are wrong. Also, try to see the personal motives of those offering it to you; find out what they want. Ask the repairman in advance what he is going to charge you.

Do not think of esoteric wisdom as being far off in some remote temple in Tibet. It is as close as your own mind. Let me give you an example of how you can save yourself. Suppose you are exchanging letters with someone. He owes you the next letter, which fails to come, making you uncomfortable. Instead of waiting for it, write him again, not to force a letter from him, but to *deliberately crack your pride that says, "I will not write again until he replies."* This simple idea can add a million dollars to your psychic treasure chest.

Happily, one healthy esoteric insight leads to another, for instance:

If you understand the supremacy of your inner kingdom,
you will also see no need to depend upon others for happiness.
If your insight reveals that heartache is nothing more than

a particular way of thinking, it also reveals the true way to dissolve heartache.

If you see that people are cruel because they are lost, you will also see no need to fear their cruelty.

If your understanding reveals the futility of using conditioned thoughts to solve problems, you also experience tremendous relief from mental struggles.

If you see the completeness of your inner essence, you will also realize poise and calmness in exterior affairs.

"I cannot thank you enough," said Lawrence R., as he took a chair opposite me, "for explaining the process of mental movies. I now see how I unwisely permitted the unreeling of harmful mental scenes. They seem to provide a sort of painful pleasure, don't they?"

For the next hour we discussed the human mind. I explained to him that the majority of people do not have mental simplicity; they spend their hours frantically figuring out *how* to live. They mistake *thinking about life* for the *living of life*. Life is not for frantic thought, but for living itself.

As we finished our talk, Lawrence commented, "You know, you are looking at a man who has been very foolish for most of his life."

I replied, "Yes, I understand. Every step toward rightness is preceded by the insight that we did not really know what we assumed we did."

THE CONFERENCE OF THE BIRDS

Let me introduce a good example of esoteric literature of considerable value to your quest. It is the interesting classic entitled *The Conference of the Birds,* written by a Sufi teacher, Fariduddin Attar.

The story tells of a group of birds who assemble to find their king, called the Simurgh (who represents the Truth, sought by every man). The birds are led by one of their own, a hoopoe, who possesses certain spiritual insight. The hoopoe proclaims the glories of their king, making the birds eager to set out in their quest of him. Pledging their friendship to each other, they make plans for the adventurous journey.

However, with the dawning realization of the difficulties involved, each bird comes up with an excuse, according to his nature. I restate three of them in summary form, as follows.

The first bird to speak is the nightingale: *"How can I join in the journey when I already have such a great love? I love the rose, with all its fragrant petals, which provides pleasure day and night. A smile from my rose tells me all is well with myself. How can I deprive myself of a single night of rapture?"*

Replies the hoopoe, *"To be dazzled by exterior forms which soon fade away, is delusion disguised as rapture. Forsake passing sensations and seek the eternal."*

The hawk asks, *"Why should I seek another king when I am already a great favorite at my king's court? I exchange my talents as a bird of prey for the court's royal favors. My king is served by my hunting skills, and I find my own desires satisfied in return. What need have I of the Simurgh?"*

The hoopoe points out, *"The closer one is to the pleasures of an earthly king, the closer one is to his sudden wrath. How can you call your concealed uneasiness by the name of satisfaction?"*

The sparrow next pleads, *"I am a poor and plain weakling with neither the strength nor the intelligence for such a journey. Let such a humble creature as I remain in contentment in my present place."*

The hoopoe answers bluntly, *"You are not humble; you are a little hypocrite. Your vanity shows with every sickening falsehood you speak. Stop lying and start walking."*

When the birds have finished their foolish excuses, the hoopoe supplies advice and encouragement, which I also summarize:

"Do not listen with indifference to words of truth, for your very deliverance depends upon sincere attention. Give up your usual logic, for though it appears impressive in public, it is a marsh to catch the unwary. With right effort you can become your own master. Do not despair if the way seems obscure. Free yourself of the love of reputation and honors. And do not be deluded by the possession of power. Remember, when you cross over the raging river of self-love, you leave behind a thousand self-torments. So do not loiter along the way and do not give way to

self-pity. Withdraw from wandering thoughts and remain true to your own essence. In these ways you will find the great king you seek."

The birds which persisted to the end made a wondrous discovery. The great king which they sought was within themselves!

HOW TO BECOME A TRULY NEW PERSON

Imagine a man standing outdoors, who is under a hypnotic spell. The hypnotist sets a statue of hardened salt before the subject. The statue is made in the likeness of the subject. The hypnotized man is told that he *is* this statue; the figure is his very self.

Heavy rain starts to fall on the statue, causing anxiety in the subject. Assuming that the figure is his self, he races frantically around for a blanket to protect it. He curses the rain. He demands that others aid his nervous efforts. Whatever and whoever stands in the way of his efforts to protect the statue is ruthlessly shoved aside. His cruel behavior is justified by the thought, "After all, my very life is at stake. I have a right to protect myself against whatever threatens me." Whenever the rain knocks off a bit of salt, he awkwardly tries to stick it back in place, while sensing its futility.

All the while he is terrified, hostile, depressed—and hypnotized, though not realizing it.

Finally, in spite of all his efforts, the rain destroys the figure. The shock begins to awaken him, and to his amazement, he feels utterly different from the way he had fearfully anticipated he would feel. Instead of emptiness, he is fulfilled. In place of the expected terror, he has peace.

Now an enlightened man, he smiles at his former foolishness. He sees how his frantic folly was energized only by an illusion. In reality, he was protecting nothing of true value. Now, seeing things as they really are, he is a new man.

In life, the hypnotized man takes his imaginary ideas about himself as being his real self, which is untrue. It is a self made of salt, subject to dissolution by the rains of life, in the form of troubles, heartaches and shocks.

The problem is not the salt-self, but our resistance to the rains which could destroy both the salt-self and the grief it causes. By permitting the rain to do its good work of destruction, we see the falseness revealed. With this awakening, we are new.

Here is a superb method for making this book work for you: Select any problem or grief. Now, try to see it through the eyes of esoteric insight. Maybe you painfully regret some past occasion when you failed to take advantage of a certain opportunity. But esotericism says that nothing can be added to or subtracted from your true self. So you now see that the past event could have added nothing of true value to you. Another chain has fallen.

HOW TO BE HUMILIATED AND APPRECIATE IT

Whoever can find positive value in a seemingly negative condition is a truly wise individual. It can be done with every negative condition, but let's select those times when you feel shamed or humiliated.

What is humiliation? Follow closely. It is the puncturing by reality of some imaginary picture we have of ourselves. We hold a secret picture of being noble or honest or kindly, or of possessing other virtues. Something happens that proves that we have deceived ourselves, and down we fall into humiliation. Because the shame is painful to the ego, it creates other self-defeating emotions, including anger, envy and despair.

Now, we can find positive value in humiliation by accepting it, that is, by voluntarily permitting the humiliation to run its full course. We must neither resist nor resent it. The pain in humiliation exists in the gap between the fact and the fancy about ourselves. By allowing humiliation to have its own way, the gap disappears, and so does pain. *"Then faults turn to good, because they humiliate without discouraging."* (François Fénelon)

How Accepted Humiliation Enriches

When discussing these ideas with Ellen A., our dialogue went like this:

"How does accepted humiliation enrich us?" she asked.

"Suppose you quarrel with someone whom you must meet the next day. Your first tendency will be to cling to your original attitudes in order to maintain ego-centered wishes to be right. This need to be right is based on a fearful need to preserve a fictitious identity of being a right person. But if you voluntarily sacrifice this self-centered need, if you go through the shock of giving it up, you will be free of its fear and pain."

"So with what attitudes do I meet this person?"

"With nothing from memory. Your new attitudes will be without motive, desire or nervousness. Having nothing to defend, you have no argument with the other person. Your free self handles everything calmly and skillfully, regardless of the other person's attitude. You must experience this to grasp it."

"So I am really accepting the destruction of my false notions about myself?"

"Exactly. And when that happens, great relief appears. You need no longer bear the burden of planning and memorizing future actions. Instead, your inner essence acts for you with new wisdom and accuracy. Recall how Jesus told his disciples that they need not think of what to say when standing before their accusers. He was referring to this psychic spontaneity that speaks and lives for us."

Ellen sat there quietly for a few moments. Her very silence indicated fresh understanding.

THE ADVANTAGES OF DESTROYING YOUR ILLUSIONS

You see, Truth, Reality, God—call it what you wish—is out to destroy the illusions we have about ourselves. This is the same as saying that Truth is out to rob us of our suffering, for pain arises from illusion and from no other place.

If I conceitedly enjoy the reputation of being a decent and respectable citizen, and if I permit unexpected disgrace to destroy my enjoyment, I have broken through a foolish dream-state to come closer to mental rest.

If I am hoping for the appearance of an exciting or beneficial event, and meet its non-appearance without complaint, I am becoming emotionally mature.

If I am an important and honored person in the professional world, and voluntarily agree to the new and unimportant circumstances of retirement, I will not suffer.

If I love to believe that I am a reasonable and intelligent person, and permit some stupid blunder to indicate otherwise, I am gaining true intelligence.

Who can understand and profit from all this? Whoever is genuinely interested in doing so.

On one occasion, several members of my lecture audience asked to come the next day to discuss various questions. Here are four of the questions and answers:

Q. Can you provide an example of a shocking truth which we sense as true, but hesitate to admit?

A. Psychologically, there is no difference between your best friend and your worst enemy, unless your friend happens to be the one-in-a-million awakened man.

Q. I feel that my life is motiveless, without purpose.

A. Why do you think you must have a motive for doing something? Why can't you simply follow an event, easily and spontaneously, merely because it presents itself to you?

Q. Is it true or false that everything works for our good?

A. If you are really working on yourself, it is true, but not otherwise. For example, if you realize how unaware you were of yourself for the last few hours, the seeing of that defeat is success.

Q. I would like to know the advantages offered by esotericism.

A. Would you call genuine happiness an advantage?

YOUR INSIGHT BANISHES ALL HUMAN STRUGGLING

Many readers found the following ideas to be both helpful and encouraging. They appeared in my book, *The Power of Your Supermind:*

> *More and more our sincere seeker realizes his need to do nothing except to be an aware person from moment to moment. In one flash of insight he banishes the awful compulsion to scheme, protect, avoid, revise, attack, grab, cling, retreat, resist, regret, worry, expect, struggle, insist, demand,*

crave, battle, blame, apologize, persuade, believe. The whole terrible burden is cleared away. In its place he has quiet awareness.[1]

It is quite possible for a man to declare, "I refuse to ever fear anything any more," and really mean it. But this can come only when he has seen something, when his declaration includes, "I will not be afraid, even if I must plunge fully into my fear, and let it consume me if it must." It *must* consume him, and his very willingness to let it be so, is what makes his declaration true. The consuming of his supposed-self is the consuming of the fear itself.

Truth, Reality, God, cannot be found with that part of the mind we call memory. What does this mean? It means that Truth is not an idea or belief we acquired in an attempt to feel secure or to identify ourselves as people with solid convictions. Happiness is not found in acquired ideas, even if those ideas seem pious. Happiness comes through living fully with each present moment, with no reference to either past or future.

In most cases, when a man thinks he is praying or meditating, he is merely muttering a familiar lullaby which he hopes will put his anxieties to sleep for awhile. But there is true meditation which consists of honest self-study, and reflection upon esoteric ideas.

There is a vast difference between reading about esoteric truths and actually living from them. The difference is between true happiness and counterfeit happiness. A man could read a hundred books about banking, visit the stock exchange every day, talk and write about finances, and still not have a cent of his own. This means that the less the distance between private thoughts and public behavior, the greater the happiness.

There is a well of life-saving wisdom, but you must personally lower your bucket.

HOW TO ATTAIN AUTHENTIC LOVE AND PEACE

Gustav Meyrink, whose writings delve deeply into the esoteric world, compares men with slips of paper which flutter about the

---

[1] Vernon Howard, *The Power of Your Supermind* (West Nyack, N.Y.: Parker Publishing Company, Inc., 1967).

village square. Driven by the wind, they chase each other, collide, separate again. They become calm as the wind dies down, giving an appearance of an armistice, but a moment later they whirl about once more.

If the slips could speak like men, they would no doubt claim they were not only moving under their own will, but were performing helpful and intelligent actions. Thinking of themselves as dictators, they are, in fact, dictated to by the slightest breeze.

In other words, *the unawakened individual does not belong to himself.* He belongs to his mechanical habits, which he calls his personality; he belongs to his sexual passions which he labels as signs of manhood. He belongs to his clutching fears and to his idiotic devotions, to his compulsions to please the boss and impress the neighbor. He belongs to his illusory ideas, but not to himself, which creates a gulf between him and the very peace he seeks.

What can he do? He can become aware that he *needlessly* belongs to his own sorrow.

People sometimes ask me, "But why pay so much attention to sorrow? Why not dwell on happy things, like love and peace?"

It is because happy things cannot come until we face and pass through the fact of sorrow. Otherwise, we have an imaginary happiness, which is soon consumed, like flowers falling into a fireplace. Everyone is much more deeply involved with suffering than he likes to admit. He sees it only when his desires and demands are refused by reality, which forces him to see his frustrations.

Reader, think for a moment. *Is* there love or peace on earth, or is there conflict and cruelty? Which more accurately describes human existence? But because human beings refuse to face this simple fact, for fear there is no solution, they set up idealistic labels of "love" and "peace." But these are merely labels, words, ideas, not actual states. So we have let labels shield us from seeing the prevalence of sorrow in our world. Consequently, we are prevented from studying the problem with intelligence and understanding.

Can we see this simple contradiction of *talking* about love, while *dwelling* in no such state? This should be the most obvious fact on earth to us. If we will bear the shock of seeing this contradiction, *first in ourselves,* we would open the door to something entirely new, including authentic love and peace.

SUMMARY OF OUTSTANDING POINTS IN THIS CHAPTER

1. Study esoteric ideas as the good news they are.
2. Do not hesitate to abandon useless procedures.
3. Inner power is as close as your own mind.
4. What you seek is now within you.
5. You can become a totally new person.
6. Accepted humiliation is a never-failing teacher.
7. Cosmic riches are for all who want them.
8. Make esotericism a daily experience.
9. With new insight, you can belong to yourself.
10. Genuine love and peace come with inward newness of spirit.

15

The Inner Perceptive
Way to Solve Painful
Problems of Living

Problems exist in a conditioned mind—which is a faulty mind—and nowhere else.

You wonder about it? Let us examine it.

You failed to get what you wanted, so now you have a problem, a conflict, a frustration. What was it you failed to get? A new friend, a reward, an honor, a sale? Maybe you failed to persuade someone to go along with you, or maybe you missed in your attempt to influence an event to satisfy your desire. Whatever it was, you failed to get what you wanted, and so the pain arose.

Why did it not pain your neighbor? Why is he free of your problem?

Because he did not falsely value it as you did. He will be pained by his own conditioned values, but he may think you are quite foolish for wanting that scheming woman or that hypocritical man or that fickle friend. He is blissfully free of your painful problem because he did not attribute false value to it in the first place.

Would you like more evidence? Something closer to home? Think of that person or event which caused you so much grief a day or month or year ago. Where is the grief now? Do you begin to see?

If you do not have false values you cannot have false problems. Yes, the problems themselves are false, for they come from

179

a faulty mind, just as flat loaves of bread come from a faulty oven.

Where are we? Right back where we started. Get rid of our wrong ways of thinking through intelligent work, and problems no longer exist. You can perform all sorts of mental magic like this as you advance in esoteric wisdom.

There is something entirely different about you which you hardly suspect. It is something of enormous value. This book points out the need for first seeing that something is seriously wrong with us, for example, that we live for foolish acquisitions. However, once that is accomplished, we come to the truth. We taste new powers for true happiness.

HOW ONE MAN CONQUERED HIS PROBLEMS

Carl J. stated his problem like this: "I envied ambitious and successful people, and wondered why I could not be like them. I thought something was wrong with me because I had not achieved very much. In spite of every effort I made, nothing turned out right. I worked, studied, planned, did everything you are supposed to do in order to reach the top. Nothing happened, except more envy and discouragement on my part.

"Then," Carl continued, "I came across some of the ideas that you, Mr. Howard, have been teaching. I confess I did not understand your books at first, but there was a certain fascination about the ideas that I could not dismiss from my mind. I would set your books aside, only to be mysteriously drawn back to them. I now know what was going on. I was at the point in my life where I wanted, above all else, to know what life was really all about. And I was willing to start a patient and persistent search.

"The answers came. Not all at once, for I had much thicker fog in my mind than I had supposed. For the first time I saw how little I understood. What a mass of false assumptions pressed me down! It was somewhat humiliating, but what relief to toss aside my pretense of wisdom. Finally, I broke through the nagging problem that had started my search in the first place. I saw clearly that the so-called successful men whom I had envied were total failures in obtaining happiness of life. What I had assumed was admirable ambition was nothing more than nervous compulsion. They could not have stopped their chasing if their lives depended upon it. And no sooner did they achieve one goal than they were driven to chase another.

"That, Mr. Howard, is no way to live. At last I see. Now, I place self-command first of all, not the nervous pursuit of what can never satisfy. Oh, I still have lots of discoveries to make; I realize that. But I have broken through, and I'll never go back to the old, miserable ways. Envy is no longer a torment. The pain is gone forever. So now I am stepping forward to new conquests; the only kind with real meaning."

YOU CAN COMMAND YOUR OWN LIFE

Suppose someone handed you a number of disks of glass, each the size of a saucer. Across the surface of each was printed a word—*Fear, Tension, Dejection, Sorrow.* The person handing you the disks appeared to be strong and authoritative, so you listened timidly as he instructed, "You must look at life through these disks of glass, while reacting according to the words printed on them. For example, if you see an event through the glass of *Tension,* you must respond to it with tension. Whatever the word dictates, you must automatically obey."

Assuming that this is the only way to live, you meekly follow orders. You see life through one glass after another, reacting according to the negative words. As unhappy as it makes you, you feel compelled to continue. Even when the so-called authority goes away, the negative habit continues automatically.

But one day you get tired of unhappiness. You smash the glasses. Great day! All is well! You realize that when events are seen through the eyes of reality, they are not frightening in themselves. Fear arose only because you saw things in the wrong way. The events were not negative—*you* were negative. But now you know better, and all is truly right.

Men and women, in their mechanical reactions to life, are unaware that they see life through the dictatorial glasses of falsehood. Not one man in a thousand will believe the enlightened teachers who try to explain the error. But the person who truly wishes to smash out, can do so.

That is why this book was written. I am attempting to smash the habitual glasses which make us see things with distortion, for that is what makes us right at last.

Here are some questions from one inquirer:

Q. My problem is daily pressure.

A. If you will accept pressure, when others refuse it, you will be the one who is forever free of pressure. No man ever won a contest by refusing it. Pressure exists only in an unenlightened mind.

Q. How can we break harmful habits?

A. Habits are unconscious and mechanical, so you must make them conscious. If you have the habit of nervous haste, deliberately move slowly. This makes you uncomfortable, which forces you to observe the habit. With full awareness, it falls away.

Q. I am bursting with a hundred questions!

A. By enduring the tension of your questions, and not escaping through shallow comforts, the questions themselves will disappear, along with their tension.

HOW BLUNDERS CAN TURN INTO ADVANCEMENTS

Lucy W. complained, "I want people to stop bothering me. It seems as if everyone pours their gripes onto me."

With insight, Lucy can free herself of this particular people-problem. She must see that the people in her private life are there because she asked for them in one way or another. With this insight she will cease to attract new problem-people. Along with this she must see through her own false needs for the company of problem-people. Yes, her own false needs attract them. Weakness attracts weakness, for each hopes to get something from the other. Fresh psychic strength is the answer. This means that Lucy must willingly enter her loneliness, for once others see that they cannot get anything from her, they will depart. But on the other side of this voluntary loneliness is understanding, where loneliness is impossible.

"I know this doesn't mean I must become a hermit," Lucy commented.

"No, it means to be in the social sea like a strong ship which cannot be sunk by the lashing waves."

A man may attend a thousand meetings where the topics of truth and reality and insight are discussed, but do you know what the problem is? He comes out of a meeting the very same person he was before. Nothing has changed internally.

To change, he must voluntarily release everything requiring change. If a cake of ice is brought close to a fire, it takes time to melt and warm up its water. If snow is brought, it takes less time. If water is brought close to a fire, it warms up at once. The less fixed and hard we are, the faster we warm to the light of truth.

The way is clear enough. Do we want to walk it? That is the only question. What is the way? It is to:

> Remember the necessity of waking up.
> Use all happenings for self-illumination.
> Refuse false and shallow comfort.
> Seek first the inner kingdom.

Be neither surprised nor dismayed by your hundreds of blunders along the way. Walk on. Remember that *conscious blunders* are advancements. This means to sense the wrongness of an act or attitude, even while doing it.

And have no concern for the many things not understood as yet. Attend only to your very next step, giving it all your attention, whether it be reading for knowledge or reflecting for understanding.

HOW TO BE FREE OF DAMAGING IDEAS

Man is born with the capacity for illusion, which would not be so bad if it were not for another negative factor. From the day of his birth he is bombarded by deluded adults who were themselves bombarded by their elders. So the sickness continues from one generation to another. But whoever really wants the cure can have it.

Reality constantly tries to tell us what is right, but the tricky mind distorts the message. It is like a man visiting a foreign country who asks a policeman for directions to an historic site. An interpreter comes along who offers to translate the policeman's directions for the visitor. But the interpreter stupidly and carelessly twists everything the policeman says. Not realizing what has happened, the visitor goes astray.

What are the false informations passed along by a confused mind? There are thousands of distorting messages, for instance, it is false that:

> Other human beings have real power over you.
> We can escape the penalty for self-deception.
> The past has a hold on your present.
> Self-reliance can be successfully avoided.
> Anything can prevent your supreme psychic success.

Continual attention to the psychic task at hand provides new power for self-clarity. A small child toddling across the room is distracted by a bit of colored paper or by his own shoes. The mind must concentrate its energies on the valuable journey, not on trivial distractions.

To the same degree that one is clogged to the reception of true life, one will also be clogged to the exit of false life. This means that your receptivity to the flow of spiritual and mental health will also enable you to let go of unhealthiness.

Man's complaints about the way life treats him have no justification. He is like a man who insists upon sitting in the dark, while grumbling that he cannot understand an open book before him. The opportunity to understand the truth and to profit from it must be earned by right effort, by turning on the light.

The only evil in any situation is that you have not as yet conquered it through self-conquest.

SOLVING THE PROBLEM OF SECURITY

Why should you mind if you can't find anything to do, if no one wants you, if nothing comes your way? Why should you mind the blankness? What is wrong with blankness? In your misunderstanding, you assume it represents the end of the world. However, if you would make it welcome, you would see it truly as the gate to a fantastically new world.

Take the question of security. Security is present when we have abandoned all need for security. People assume that the various anchors to which they attach themselves will prevent harmful drifting, but they don't see that the very anchors they depend upon are the weights preventing spontaneous motion. Life is motion, but it is not our personal motion. We do not move life; it moves us. As we voluntarily join the cosmic flow, we are in harmony, and therefore safe and happy.

Two men journeyed in the dark with a single lantern between them. Coming to a fork in the road, the owner of the lantern turned left, while the other hesitantly faced to the right. The man with the lantern advised his companion, "Go back for your own lantern, for then you will be fearless."

To understand something means to know it *all by yourself.*

Let's take a perfect example of how esoteric understanding sets you free from painful problems. Whenever you decide to abandon false notions, a sense of guilt arises. This guilt is absolutely false, so you must ignore it and plunge ahead. All false ideas and false systems cruelly try to keep you a slave by making you feel guilty. As if you should feel guilty over abandoning poisoned water! As you persist with your understanding, guilt gradually loses its grip and finally falls away.

If you ever feel that esoteric facts are undermining your old beliefs, I am very glad for you. This is an essential and a progressive step.

Here are questions asked at one of my lectures:

Q. Some parts of me are actively attracted to esoteric ideas, but other parts are indifferent. What can be done with the lazy ones?

A. Just be aware of them and continue to work.

Q. Do I really have a choice in life, or not? Some teachings say yes, others say no.

A. You have the choice to drop the false assumption that you presently have choice. By penetrating this esoteric mystery you will see that there is no difference between your choice and that of God, Truth, Nature, call it what you like. You and Life are One, which is peace.

Q. I am applying esoteric principles to a bad habit of mine. How can I know if I am making progress?

A. When you cease to wonder about progress. Your wondering is a form of anxiety, and where anxiety exists, there is not the necessary understanding.

A WONDER-WORKING STATEMENT TO MAKE

Remarked Randy J., who was attending my lectures, "I see what you mean when you describe human beings as hypnotized. I have friends who don't see the slightest connection between their mental viewpoints and their muddled lives. I'm not being self-righteous, either; I know how long I fought the principles we are learning at these lectures. What can be done to lower our resistance to the liberating facts?"

This led us to a general discussion of helpful ideas, which I summarize for you in the following paragraphs.

No man ever succeeds in covering up that awful ache he feels inside, no matter what he tries, and he tries everything. He shoves it out the front door and it sneaks in the back. He might as well give up, and whether he senses it or not, his giving up, his voluntary defeat, is the very victory he wishes. He must be aware that everything he has done up to now has been a useless pretense. That is enough, for from that fertile ground can blossom what is real.

How can we find a problem-free life? There is a way.

If you have never deliberately questioned yourself, now is the time. Ask yourself, "What is my life all about? Where am I going? What do I really want? Isn't there more to this existence than making money and involvement in noisy activities and one confusion after another? What is the purpose of my life?"

This is a healthy process, for it brings to the surface your subconscious questions. The average man is like a lost hiker who pretends not to notice that he passes the same landmark every few hours. Self-inquiry destroys such self-deception, making the true path visible.

It is not shameful to lack the answers, for that condition is merely an absence of understanding which you can remedy. What is shameful is not to know, while pretending to know. We can brush gold paint onto a burned out light bulb, but it will still not give light.

There is a certain mental statement you can make which works wonders. It must be said calmly, unemotionally, as a simple statement of fact. That statement is, *"I don't know."* Having said it, you must leave it right there, making no effort to do anything about your not-knowing. Do not desire to know, for that opens the trapdoor through which will sneak all sorts of deceitful mental imps who pretend that they know. And that puts you right back where you started.

Say, "I don't know," and leave it right there. You are doing what is truly right and helpful.

HOW TO SIMPLIFY YOUR DAY

Poor, pathetic little man. If he wasn't so tragic he would be funny. Here is a man conniving for security by building up the very temporary possessions which make him feel insecure. And there goes his wife, striving for all the pleasure she can get, totally unaware of the pain in her very striving.

Nothing but our own illusions compels us to run so hard. With awareness of the illusions we can cease to run. We have no place to go anyway; we are already there, but don't see it. The teachings of Zen make this clear.

One of the most difficult tasks of the freedom-seeker is to do nothing, but this *doing nothing in the esoteric sense is the doing of everything needful.* Humanity can be likened to couples dancing outdoors in a thunderstorm, with everyone pretending that they are dancing to music. Only when they stop to see their actual condition can intelligent action take place. To change from where we are, we must first see where we are.

How unnecessarily do human beings complicate things! They worry over a thousand problems, thus forcing themselves into a frantic search for a thousand solutions.

There are not thousands of problems—just one: Man dwells in a state of psychic sleep, of which he is totally unaware.

Consequently, there is no need to waste life in chasing pseudo-solutions. There is only one solution, namely, to awaken from the nightmare. With this, the very source of our problems is smashed.

You may ask, "All right, I suspect I may have been asleep all my life, but what can I do to shake myself awake?"

What can you do?

> *Whenever you see other people making themselves sick and tired by the wrong use of their minds, you can determine not to live like that.*
>
> *You can see that your real self has no need whatsoever for either defense or offense.*
>
> *Whenever you are in anguish, you can see that it is simply because your mind is hypnotically paying attention to the wrong thing.*
>
> *You can realize that no pleasant fancy on earth is as beneficial to you as an unpleasant fact.*
>
> *Whenever you fail to hear cosmic harmony, you can realize that the music is always playing, but you fail to hear it because of your distance from the orchestra.*
>
> *In those flashing moments when you see things clearly, you can notice how the truth harmonizes with your own natural sensibleness.*

HOW TO WIN NEW STRENGTH AND SELF-CONFIDENCE

Fred B. came to seek new strength to battle his way out of the problems he had finally faced. "After hearing your lectures," he said, "I have fresh hope. But I know how easily I give up. How can I maintain the strength to keep going until I break through?"

I asked, "Do you have a major problem just now, or a collection of small ones?"

His pause indicated hesitation in speaking of what was on his mind, but he finally said, "I feel guilty toward those I have wronged in past years. How can I ever make things right?"

"Forgiveness is not necessarily a matter of going to these people, but of psychic understanding. You must forgive yourself for being spiritually asleep; this is possible when you see things as they really are. This pardons you from every offense you have ever committed, for you knew not what you did; you were out of your true mind. Forgiveness has nothing to do with the offended person; it is solely a matter of your own awakening. This will become increasingly clear to you."

"And I will be free of guilt today?"

"If you sweep out yesterday's trash today, is the room clean today?"

"And the new strength I need will also come?"

"Psychic insight *is* your strength. There is no other."

Fred and I continued our discussion of new strength and self-confidence with the following ideas.

Most people live patched-up lives, like a gardener with a leaky hose. The water which could refresh the garden is drained by leaks. And no matter how quickly he plugs up one leak, another breaks out. So it is with those who do not live by esoteric principles. The ample power of their psychic system is dissipated in hundreds of leaks, including irritability, bad habits, sex neuroses.

Esoteric insight becomes an entirely new channel which supplies tremendous psychic energy, which was there all the time, but wasted.

One helpful principle of esotericism is to use every happening for new strength. Suppose a woman has her feelings hurt. How can this build psychic muscle? Let's investigate. What really hurts is that the unpleasant event produced self-doubt. Now, this kind of self-doubt is positive, beneficial, for it forces the woman to see that she was depending upon fictitious self-strength. It *was* fictitious, else she would not have been shaken. Having seen her false stand, she can abandon it, making room for the true.

THE SURE CURE FOR ALL HUMAN PROBLEMS

It is no tragedy to lose money or health or friend or reputation. What is tragic is to fail to use these happenings to grow in cosmic self-strength. True heroes do not run away. They stand bravely, in spite of all which threatens to destroy them. And I will tell you something. If you will let what is trying to destroy you succeed completely, you will come to the point where you can never be destroyed again.

Stop placing an habitual evaluation on whatever happens to you. Observe it impartially, just as if it happened to someone else. The secret is to withdraw the usual sense of "I" from the happening, for this false self distorts everything into pain or counterfeit pleasure. When you cease to evaluate, you rise above both pain and false pleasure, to quietness.

The next time you have an unpleasant experience, ask yourself, "How would I feel if I had wanted it to happen just as it did?" This can start a new way of thinking, which is your esoteric aim.

It is a great mistake to think that you are at the mercy of the human jungle—of the economic system, cruel people, hypocritical laws and of human stupidity in general. You simply do not realize that the prison bars exist in your mind only.

Nothing whatsoever is pressing you down except that which wrongly exists within your own psychic system.

What is the cause of human problems? A false sense of self is the parent of all conflicts. And since troubles cease with the fading of the false self, this is a happy fact we can work on. Society cannot help us in this great task, for the whole social structure is founded upon illusions of self-grandeur, breeding cruelty and hypocrisy.

Life has its own natural, untroubled flow, quite independent of the false feeling of "I" we put into it. This flow can be neither created nor blocked, but it can be misunderstood, causing grief. We are already within the Easy Flow of life, but do not see it because of ego-interference. We increasingly enjoy what is already ours by the steady reduction of the false self.

CHAPTER SUMMARY OF IMPORTANT IDEAS

1. Esoteric intelligence will solve all painful problems.
2. You can see life in a fresh and pleasant way.
3. All difficulties can be changed into advancements.
4. The way out of problems is ready for all who want to understand.
5. We must rid our minds of false notions.
6. A return to your true nature produces real security.
7. To admit not knowing the answers is the start of genuine wisdom.
8. A thousand problems can be solved with a single esoteric insight.
9. Esoteric insight is true and constant self-strength.
10. You are never at the mercy of anyone or anything.

16

Secrets
for Magical Daily
Successes

When a man falls into grief, he wants to know two things: "What caused this? How can I escape it?"

The answer is so simple that he may miss it: "You caused it. Change yourself."

There is the human level and there is the esoteric level. When a man transfers his life from the human level to the esoteric level, he lives in both with ease. But whoever lives only on the human plane, has nothing but grief, for that is the constant condition of that plane.

I talk with many businessmen who want to know how esotericism can relieve strains and worries in their financial affairs. One of them, Wilbur D., began our session with, "If only I could break free of the subtle tensions of my business, my day would be a breeze. Why can't I simply conduct my affairs naturally, easily, just as I might play a game of golf?"

"You can," I told him, "when you understand your mistake."

"My mistake?"

"You identify with money. You feel good over gaining money because it seems to establish you as a certain kind of person—a success, a clever salesman. But this exposes you to the possibility of the opposite occurring: the loss of money, leaving you without any identification. Do you see this much?"

"I'm trying. It makes sense." Wilbur paused for a moment

to reflect, then said, "I can connect this with what you said in your lecture the other night. In other words, if I have ego-excitement over scoring a financial success, I will also be at the mercy of financial failure."

"Exactly. At the present time, you can see only the successful side of the swing of these opposites, because it provides excitement. When you can see both the excitement of gaining, and the pain of losing *at the same time,* you are a free man."

We fell into a discussion of the Third Way of Thinking, which is above these opposites of excitement and pain. By wishing to know these things, Wilbur is showing true intelligence. It does not take brightness to make a lot of money, but it takes real brightness to find freedom from financial tensions.

Here is a helpful story which summarizes the principles of this book. You might call it an esoteric adventure story, entitled:

THE ALARM CLOCK EXPERT

There was once a country where everyone was unhappy. Because of their misery, they sought for another land in which to live. In their search they heard of a land of bliss, called the New Nation.

However, a baffling barrier existed between their country and the New Nation. A long stretch of Dark Woods separated the two. It was rumored that the woods was filled with unknown terrors. Few people had ever penetrated it for more than a few hundred yards. Nevertheless, the very best minds in the country went to work to find ways to cross the Dark Woods and reach the New Nation.

Immediately, they discovered a severe weakness in their own natures. Because of their unhappiness and their endless quarrels, they tired quite easily, and it was necessary to stay awake until the Dark Woods were crossed. Those attempting to make the crossing fell asleep soon after entering. So because of their inclination to doze, along with their fear of the Dark Woods, few citizens ever made a serious attempt to reach the New Nation.

Still, they desperately wanted to cross, so they held a great meeting. One of their leaders spoke, "Our chief problem is our weakness of falling asleep so easily. Let's invent a special kind of alarm clock that will go off at unexpected times. That should keep us awake long enough to cross the Dark Woods."

Another citizen remarked, "I have heard of an alarm clock expert who lives in the mountains. It is said that he knows how to build individual alarm clocks. Let's invite him down here to teach us."

The invitation was instantly agreed upon. But it was not easy to persuade the alarm clock expert to come down. Indeed, he tested their sincerity by refusing the first few invitations. But finally, after persistent pleas, he consented to show them how to build individual alarm clocks. The entire country rejoiced.

But at this point, some other peculiar characteristics began to appear in the trapped citizens. Although the entire country was invited to the first lecture by the alarm clock expert, only about half attended. And some of them admitted that they came only out of curiosity. The other half of the population expressed great regret over their absence, quickly explaining that it was due to unexpected emergencies.

But those who attended, heard some interesting information. The expert mentioned some of the great Alarm Clock Experts of the past, including Jesus, Buddha and Socrates. And some of his words were painful to them; for example, he explained that most people, while giving lip-service to the New Nation, did not really want to make the journey. Man is lazy, hypocritical, and he lies about everything. All the same, the alarm clock expert cheerfully added, those who really want to cross the Dark Woods can certainly do so.

At one meeting, he supplied specific instructions for building personal alarm clocks: "The alarm clock you need is within your own mind. By repairing its faults, it can keep you awake long enough to reach the New Nation. Now, there are certain rules for making it an effective instrument. First, you must clearly see your own inability to stay awake. Then, you must want to stay awake more than you want anything else on earth. And remember, the vital parts of your alarm clock are sincerity, honesty, persistence and courage."

Strangely, the longer the meetings continued, the fewer came to listen. Among those who stayed away were the leaders of the country, the very ones who had first pleaded for aid from the expert. Some of them even angrily denounced him, and went off to start their own groups, while advertising themselves as experts. They attracted many followers, who soon quarreled among themselves.

But to the few who remained, the teacher imparted further counsel:

"Absorb as many esoteric truths as you can. Then, at unexpected times, they will ring bells within your mind, keeping you awake. Try to see that these truths are not trying to take comfort from you, but wish to confer a new kind of comfort which cannot be shaken by anything. And beware of false prophets—as if they really care for you!"

At the final meeting, the expert gave them encouraging counsel: "There is really nothing to fear in the Dark Woods, but you cannot see this as yet. So press on, fearing nothing, avoiding nothing, welcoming every experience. The New Nation belongs to those who persist in spite of everything."

With this, the alarm clock expert returned to the mountains. Those who had listened faithfully, went to work to build their individual alarm clocks. Now knowing how to stay awake, they set out, crossed the Dark Woods, and reached the New Nation.

THE EFFECTIVE SIMPLICITY OF COSMIC STRENGTH

Note the tangible benefits of applying the simplest esoteric principles as brought out in the following questions asked by one of my students:

Q. Please provide a single good idea for winning happiness.

A. Remember that suffering is nothing more than a state of hypnosis. To break it, become aware of yourself. Whenever you suffer, with awareness look around at where you are and at what you are doing.

Q. One idea of yours helped immensely. You said I must let daily events fall on my *insight*, not on my *desires*.

A. Yes, the best kind of success story is when a man behaves like a hero when he *doesn't* get the promotion or the girl.

Q. How can I handle a terrifying situation?

A. You can try to destroy a terrifying situation, which will eventually destroy you; or you can let the situation destroy you, which eventually leaves you undestroyed.

Q. You say we should meet everything with an uncomplaining mind, but how can we live in a lunatic world without complaint?

A. Just as you always live within the weather, but don't suffer mentally unless you complain about it.

In itself, the esoteric way is really quite simple. Its simplicity becomes our simplicity with right intentions. The more you plunge into these things, the more sense they make. Let us make a grand summary of the entire life-saving process:

1. *An individual is lost from himself.*
2. *He feels, but does not understand his "lostness."*
3. *He is lost because of false ideas about himself.*
4. *If he sincerely wishes self-awakening, he can have it.*
5. *To start, he must detect and abandon false ideas.*
6. *This leads to a new sense of himself and life.*
7. *His new sensing produces an actual change of being.*
8. *He lives happily, serenely, triumphantly.*

All this is really quite beautiful. Nothing is more beautiful than breaking out. For example, fear exists only where there is false belief. If I fear external authorities, it is because I falsely believe in their power to affect me. For correction, I can see that they have power on the human level, but it is powerless to affect my psychic system which dwells on the cosmic level. No matter what they do, they do nothing that can harm me. This understanding banishes my fear once and for all.

SURE STEPS TOWARD SUPREME SUCCESS

Do not assume that you know where the path is leading you. Assumptions are based on memory, which ties you to the old, preventing the new. We don't want to remain on the same old merry-go-round, seeing the same monotonous scenes. The dropping of habitual assumptions gets you off the weary ride, letting you explore the wondrous countryside.

The secret is this: Do not try to find what you should do, but see the utter uselessness of what you usually do. Perception of the false makes way for the true.

Wherever you are, regardless of past failures, you can discover a totally new kind of self-reliance. To be self-reliant is to be halfway out of the woods. It is your pleasant task to uncover the wisdom already within you. You need not be like a man walking in the night with a lighted but covered lantern.

Be discouraged by nothing. There is nothing to fear. Though you fail a thousand times, whatever is necessary for you can be found. Your cosmic essence is stronger than anything on earth. So go to the very end of things. Do not stop short. What you want is waiting for you.

There exists an utterly new and fantastic kind of life-success. When the ego-self is out of the way, you can go anywhere and do anything with total victory. This is because you have an entirely new definition of success, unknown to those still drugged by delusion. The deluded man thinks that success consists of ego-gratification, therefore, he fears whatever clashes with his egotistical demands.

But you, with your esoteric insight, are indifferent to results. Therefore, there is no conflict between you and what happens to you. So, whatever happens is all right; it leaves you peaceful.

Work at vanquishing the false sense of self. Then, this new kind of success will come to you. Above the opposites of human success and human failure is cosmic success. It comes to those who dare to venture beyond ordinary life. Walt Whitman writes:

> It is not far, it is within reach,
> Perhaps you have been on it since you were born and did not know.

YOUR NEW KIND OF VICTORY

Lola B., who had asked to see me, was shy about coming to the point. But finally she said, "I am afraid of someone in my life. What makes him so bad?"

I explained to Lola that no one is bad by conscious choice. In his darkness, a man behaves badly because he wrongly assumes that it is essential to his psychic survival. So only consciousness can cure badness. However, since almost everyone thinks he is already conscious, wickedness continues.

Lola replied, "I have read your books and I have learned this. In simple terms, this person cannot see what he is doing to either himself or to the family he claims to love. But what can I do about my fear?"

"Use it," I told her, "as a study point. See that whoever needs to frighten you is frightened himself. Do not use the situation to make yourself a martyr. Especially, see your own false need of him. You cannot be frightened of anyone from whom you want nothing."

Later, Lola reported, "The situation continues as it was, but I am truly beginning to see it differently. You know, I feel this new kind of victory you speak about."

It is utterly useless to try to change the outer world, for it is but a reflection of inner causes. The true seeker seeks to change himself. It is as if our barefoot ancestors met in tribal council to solve the problem of the rocky ground which hurt their feet. Someone suggests a vast program of planting grass all over the world. Another suggests the planting of trees at regular intervals, so that they might swing forward from one branch to the next. Finally, comes the sensible suggestion, "Why not pad our own feet?"

When we finally see that we remain the same pained person, regardless of where we go or what we do, we lose all faith in the power of anything but the inner self to deliver us.

Inner change arises from self-awareness, and from no other place. What do we mean by self-awareness? It is really quite simple. It means to see things as they really are, not as our faulty minds distort them. So our first step toward psychic health is to see the present faultiness of the mind.

We can explore an example of faulty thinking, of non-awareness of things as they are. Here is a man with a particular non-awareness which we can call borrowed confidence. He has a lovely wife and family, comfortable surroundings and bright hopes for the future. He feels great confidence. Unfortunately, it is borrowed confidence. He has borrowed his feelings from exterior conditions which are subject to change. How will he feel when he loses them?

There is an entirely different kind of confidence taught by esotericism. It does not lean on exterior supports nor on interior expectations. It relies upon nothing but the truth within. And since this truth does not change and cannot fail, its support is solid regardless of exterior shakings.

HOW TO REFRESH YOUR DAY

We can take a simple but very practical example of self-awareness in action. Notice everything possible about your speech habits. Is the tone of your voice high or low? Do you speak slowly, swiftly, moderately? Do you have favorite phrases which are repeated quite often? Do you impatiently wait for another person to stop speaking, so that you can give your opinions?

Be aware of all this, for speech habits are connected with every human problem, such as family quarrels, sex difficulties, hounding guilts. Why? Because speech reveals the inward nature of the speaker. A frightened man shows it with his words of alarm; a woman with a critical nature reveals it with unkind speech.

By observing our speech habits, we learn valuable things about ourselves, which is the first step toward wholeness. In turn, that wholeness refreshes our day.

The following questions and answers will refresh your memory of general esoteric guidance:

Q. How can I find relief from my confusion?

A. Anyone can *relieve* confusion, which is why few people change things. Confusion, endured to the very end, destroys itself. When you anxiously try to make it go away, it merely huddles down in the cellar, to pop up at odd times.

Q. I still don't understand why I must first attend to my own development, instead of helping others. Don't I help myself by helping others?

A. Not if your sly motive is to evade responsibility for your own awakening. Suppose you and some friends are in a dark room. If you don't want the darkness, and switch on the light for yourself, your friends are included in the light.

Q. How can I grasp all this?

A. Don't be dramatic; be real. Don't seek sensation; seek truth. Don't justify yourself; study yourself.

Now that you have learned many things, reflect upon this:

Most human beings are able to dwell only in separate worlds, and in only one of these worlds at a time. Their world is either anchored or adrift, blessed or cursed, balanced or unbalanced, active or actionless, knowing or unknowing, a world where they are somebody, or a world where they are nobody. You must be able to dwell in all worlds together, and at the same moment. When doing so, all such worlds disappear, and with this miracle, nothing can ever hurt you again.

YOU CAN CERTAINLY SUCCEED

The Truth will not permit us to play with it, as a child plays with toys. It is not a plaything to be taken up or abandoned according to the mood of the moment. We may neither meddle with it nor try to change it according to our personal desires. It is what it is, and we either accept it as it is or not at all.

Harsh? As harsh as the doctor who warns us of the consequences of ignoring the medicine.

If you want to know what you value in life, notice what you get in life. They will be the same, for we always get what we truly value. If you subconsciously value a noisy kind of life, you have it, even though you say you prefer quietness. If you value social excitement over the inner kingdom, you have the excitement, even though you say you prefer the kingdom. Everyone on earth may support a lie, but your own nature won't. To change what you get, change what you value.

The problem is, many of the parts within a man *recognize* a truth when they hear it, but only one small part wants to *receive and live by it.* If a person would aid this spark of light it could grow at the expense of the dark parts which want nothing to do with the truth. So man's position is not at all hopeless. It is bright with hope, because a man can actually work on himself and for himself.

We must dig ten times deeper than we do, because the confusion is ten times deeper than we think. But if we steadfastly prefer the grand facts to shallow reassurances, we will shake ourselves free of the painful need for constant reassurances.

The story is told of a native of an island in the Pacific, whose pineapple grove was destroyed by the fires of an enemy raid. When the war ended, he stood in the middle of the ruins and looked around in all directions. He finally saw what he wanted— a small, clear space. That was all he needed. Starting with that small clearing, he pushed back the ruins to build a new grove.

Unfortunately, many people postpone life-transformation because they think a great deal is required of them. The only requirement is a single, small clearing, anywhere in the life-ruins. It can be the dawning suspicion that one has been an actor or actress, and not a real person. It can be the acceptance of the collapse of previous supports, or a willingness to drop a single false notion. It can be an urge to read esoteric literature.

Others have succeeded, and so can you.

TWO DYNAMIC PROGRAMS FOR SELF-ADVANCEMENT

`Program 1. Make it your consistent practice to combine several methods provided in this book. First, write them down on paper for constant reference. Next, put them into practice in daily living during the following weeks. As you do so, a very interesting and surprising revelation will occur: You will see how one thing connects with another, how they are *one*—which means growing insight and strength for you. For example, if you wish *daily relaxation,* you could make a list like this:

1. Stop useless thoughts which drain energy.
2. Deliberately relax tense muscles.
3. Realize the need for psychic awakening.
4. Abandon pointless activities.
5. Dare to let go!

Program 2. Remember, your pleasant task is to prove all these things for yourself. Then, they are no longer mere ideas, but powers for daily success. Use the following spaces to note your own helpful ideas. Refer to them from time to time.

1. ————————————————————————————

2. ————————————————————————————

3. ————————————————————————————

4. ————————————————————————————

5. ————————————————————————————

6. ————————————————————————————

7. ————————————————————————————

8. ————————————————————————————

9. ————————————————————————————

10. ————————————————————————————

VALUABLE POINTS IN REVIEW OF THIS CHAPTER

1. Life on the esoteric level is satisfyingly beautiful.
2. You can discover the New Nation within yourself.
3. Desire psychic awakening more than anything else.
4. Persist in esoteric understanding in spite of everything which discourages you.
5. Do not be afraid of losing your ego-supporting beliefs.
6. A new kind of life-success awaits you.
7. Self-awareness is a great power for daily success.
8. Esoteric living refreshes your day.
9. Start wherever you are, however you are.
10. Just as others have succeeded, so can you succeed.

About
VERNON HOWARD

Vernon Howard broke through to another world. He saw through the illusion of suffering and fear and loneliness. From 1965 until his death in 1992 he wrote books and conducted classes which reflect a degree of skill and understanding that may be unsurpassed in modern history. Tape recordings of many of his class talks are available.

Today more than 7 million readers worldwide enjoy his exceptionally clear and inspiring presentations of the great truths of the ages. His books are widely used by doctors, psychiatrists, psychologists, counselors, clergymen, educators and people from all walks of life. All his teachings center around the one grand theme: *"There is a way out of the human problem and anyone can find it."*

About
NEW LIFE FOUNDATION

New Life is a nonprofit organization founded by Vernon Howard in the 1970's for the distribution and dissemination of his teachings. It is for anyone who has run out of his own answers and has said to himself, "There has to be something else." These teachings *are* the something else. All are encouraged to explore and apply these profound truths—*they work!*

The Foundation's headquarters are now located in central Arizona. Classes are conducted on a regular basis throughout Arizona and in Southern California. They are an island of sanity in a confused world. The atmosphere is friendly, light and uplifting. Don't miss the opportunity to attend your first New Life class. For details on books, tapes and classes write: New Life Foundation, PO Box 2230, Pine AZ 85544.